For more than 25 years 'The R
Great' has been one of my chu
has been a great privilege to hear the word of God from the
two Marks (Ruston and Ashton) and to fellowship with them
in the work of the Gospel. But it has also been wonderful to
keep watching the growth and development of the lives and
ministries of the members of this great church and to witness the
generations of students who have been enriched by their years in
Cambridge by belonging to such a fellowship. I trust this book
will go some way towards helping us all understand the way the
local church can be such a blessing to God's people.

PHILLIP JENSEN
The Dean of Sydney at St Andrew's Cathedral

This book is both challenging and inspiring. Mark Ashton's
eight convictions at the start and the emphasis throughout on
the centrality and power of God's word are vitally important
for all churches in any setting. For me personally, it was also
a thrilling opportunity to remember with gratitude all I owe
under God to the ministries of the two Marks at the Round
Church in Cambridge.

VAUGHAN ROBERTS
Rector of St Ebbe's, Oxford and Director of the Proclamation Trust

Principles in this book will transfer to any university town. It's
the story of a local church which invests in students, keeps world
mission firmly in view, steers through a major building project,
and plants churches. Readers will find themselves reaching for
a pencil, to look at sections again. The rich legacy of the two
Marks and their Christ-centred ministries will continue on
through these pages, by prompting stimulating and edifying
discussion.

JULIA CAMERON
Director of Publishing, The Lausanne Movement

This whole book is filled with anecdotal wisdom concerning
the principles and practice of leading a faithful local church
consistently to the praise of the Lord Jesus. If you only read
Mark Ashton's eight convictions about the local church you will

get a wonderful return, for it is a rich seam of gold. As well as being thought-provoking, this book will warm your heart and encourage you to keep labouring in the Master's harvest field.

SIMON PILCHER
Chief Executive, Fixed Income, M & G Investments

This is a deeply searching and instructive read for anyone concerned to see how a local church should be shaped by Scripture in its life and outreach. While those who know and love the Round Church, St Andrew the Great and these two fine leaders will not want to miss it, the book has a great deal to say to those who have no Cambridge connections but want to see Christ honoured in his church.

JULIAN HARDYMAN
Senior Pastor, Eden Baptist Church, Cambridge

It is worth buying this wonderful little book just to read Mark Ashton's eight convictions about the local church. Two of them – the primacy of consecutive expository preaching, and a willingness to sacrifice for the sake of others – get to the heart of how this remarkable church has managed to contribute so much to the health of the Cambridge Inter-Collegiate Christian Union for half a century. Mark Ruston and Mark Ashton demonstrated how much they value the CICCU – not with mere lip-service, but with sacrificial instincts that prompted them to put the long-term health and future of the CICCU above the temptation simply to multiply their own student programmes. The two Marks then, and Alasdair Paine now, realised that as they built up their congregations with consecutive expository preaching and sent the students back into their own college mission fields to live and speak for Jesus, the impact on Cambridge and the wider world would be greater.

The godly character and faithful ministry of these two remarkable men shines through the pages. Both of them shunned personal glory and empire-building for the love of their Lord and the building of His Kingdom. I commend it wholeheartedly.

RICHARD CUNNINGHAM
Director of UCCF: The Christian Unions

Christmas, 2012

Dear Ted and Roxanne,

PERSISTENTLY
PREACHING
CHRIST

Fifty years of Bible ministry
in a Cambridge church

Compiled and Edited by
Christopher Ash, Mary Davis and Bob White

Thank you for persistently preaching
Christ by the way you live your
lives each and every day. We are
thankful to God for the gift of
your love and friendship in our lives.
This book tells the story of The Round
church in Cambridge which is a part
of "our story." It is our prayer that
you will be blessed by this church's
history which is clearly part of
His-story. In His love +

MENTOR

Ours, Dick + Marilyn

To Fiona Ashton with
warm appreciation and love

With gratitude to God for the lives and ministries of:

Mark Ruston (1916–1990)
Vicar of the Round Church (Church of the Holy Sepulchre)
between 1955 and 1987

and

Mark Ashton (1948–2010)
Vicar of the Round Church and St Andrew the Great
between 1987 and 2010

Copyright © Mary Davis 2012

ISBN 978-1-84550-982-8

First published in 2012
in the
Mentor Imprint
by
Christian Focus Publications Ltd,
Geanies House, Fearn, Ross-shire
IV20 1TW, Scotland
www.christianfocus.com

Cover design by Daniel van Straaten

Printed by Bell and Bain, Glasgow

Contents

APPENDIX
PERSONAL REFLECTIONS

Preface

This book is about what God has done through people. Just as it was an encouragement to the believers when Paul and Barnabas 'reported everything God had done through them' (Acts 15:4), so we hope it will be an encouragement to read what God has done through one particular church fellowship in Cambridge, England, over more than half a century.

This fellowship used to be called 'The Round Church' after the building where the church met for many centuries. In 1994 the church moved to the newly restored building of St Andrew the Great and took the name 'The Round Church at St Andrew the Great'. This rather cumbersome title is intended to convey both the continuity of the new congregation with those who had previously met in the Round Church building and the fact that the church is the people rather than the building.

We have tried to paint a picture of what God has done through this church fellowship and, in particular, through two exceptional and very different ministers, Mark Ruston (vicar from 1955 until his retirement in 1987) and Mark Ashton (vicar from 1987 until his death in 2010). These two Marks are remembered with deep affection and gratitude to God for their godliness and their fruitful and loving ministries.

But we have tried to do more than just fondly reminisce. During his final illness, Mark Ashton agreed with some hesitation to this book being compiled. His reluctance was partly because of his lifelong hatred of anything that might appear to bring glory to people (especially himself) rather than God and partly because he considered there were just too many books in the Christian marketplace that really did not deserve to be there. He was very concerned that the book, as well as recording warm memories, also include theological food for thought – about how a church conducts itself, its priorities and its methods. To this end, Mark contributed his 'Eight convictions about the local church' (Chapter 1) which set the agenda for the book. We hope we have included sufficient additional food for thought to stimulate Christians in very different contexts to think about why and how they too serve the Lord Jesus Christ and his gospel. To that end, Part 2 tells the story of this particular local church, Part 3 continues the story by focusing on different areas of ministry and, in the Appendix, a number of personal reflections are recorded.

Mary Davis (née Juckes) has done all the hard work of commissioning contributions and editing the end result. Professor Bob White and I have contributed in an advisory capacity. We are grateful to God for all who have contributed, but above all for his wonderful grace in saving sinners and building Christ's church. It has been a privilege for each of us to be a part of this work at different times. We thank God for the promise of the Lord Jesus to build his church all over the world, and trust him for the future of St Andrew the Great as the unchanging gospel continues to be faithfully preached.

Christopher Ash
2012

Part i

The Local Church

Writing in the final months of his life before his death from cancer, Mark Ashton passes on his convictions about the priorities for the local church. [1]

Chapter i

Mark Ashton's
Eight convictions about the local church

This book is a modest affair. It is not an attempt to paint the last fifty years of the Round Church at St Andrew the Great in glowing colours. It is rather a celebration of the ordinariness of dogged, persistent Bible ministry in a local church setting.

It might be objected that the Round Church (or the Church of the Holy Sepulchre, to give it its official title) at St Andrew the Great in Cambridge is not an ordinary local church, being a city-centre, student church. There is certainly some truth in that. No local church is entirely ordinary. Every church has its own specific characteristics, some advantageous, some disadvantageous. Being in the centre of a city, without any parish to speak of, the St Andrew the Great building is hard for the congregation to reach, with parking increasingly restricted and expensive even on a Sunday. There are also a number of alternative churches of all sorts only a few streets away.

Being a student church does have benefits, but the student ministry is also a big drain on the resources of the church. Students are hungry for Bible teaching and require a lot of pastoral care, but their financial circumstances are such that they can contribute very little themselves toward the costs of their own ministry. Moreover, students are always leaving! In the student work we lose up to thirty percent of the congregation every year. Every summer, the final-year undergraduate students, on whom the church has poured resources for the preceding three or four years, graduate and leave Cambridge.

Like all other churches, the Round Church at St Andrew the Great has a particular blend of opportunities and challenges, advantages and handicaps. But it is the contention of this book that the ministry there has been ordinary; normal rather than exceptional. Ordinary in the sense that, while the Lord is remarkable, the ministry that has gone on at the Round Church has been an ordinary, unremarkable, routine business of regular Bible teaching, while the Holy Spirit has been at work, convicting people of sin and changing lives.

That ministry has been based upon a number of convictions, which have grown up over time, and which are outlined and explained in the rest of this chapter. They are neither exhaustive nor prescriptive. Not all of them would have been owned by my predecessor Mark Ruston, but they are in line with his ministry. My years of leadership were the natural and logical development of his thirty-two years of ministry. Indeed it was my intention when I became vicar in 1987 to maintain at all costs the inheritance I had received from my predecessor.

So this book is not a triumphant account of success. There is plenty of Christian publishing about how churches can be successful. There are some excellent books on the doctrine of the church and on how to lead a church in a biblical way. This book is neither purely theological nor purely practical. It is inevitably somewhat anecdotal. But it is our hope that reflecting on half a century in the life of a local church and on some of the convictions that have shaped this piece of history, will encourage others to persevere in ordinary local church ministry, trusting God to keep his word.

> *For since in the wisdom of God the world through its wisdom did not know him, God was pleased through the foolishness of what was preached to save those who believe. Jews demand miraculous signs and Greeks look for wisdom, but we preach Christ crucified: a stumbling block to Jews and foolishness to Gentiles, but to those whom God has called, both Jews and Greeks, Christ the power of God and the wisdom of God. For the foolishness of God is wiser than man's wisdom, and the weakness of God is stronger than man's strength (1 Cor. 1:21–25).*

Mark Ashton
November 2009

Eight convictions about the local church

These eight convictions are not intended to be an exhaustive account of how a church should run, but they are distinctive characteristics of the ministry of this particular church, and I dare to think they are sufficiently normative (as well as normal) that they may be a help to others.

1. *BIBLE: The word of God does the work of God through the Spirit of God in the people of God*

2. *LOCAL CHURCH: The local church is the primary place where the Kingdom of Heaven impacts the kingdoms of this world*

3. *EXPOSITORY PREACHING: Consecutive expository preaching by the pastor-teacher is the best normal diet of the local church*

4. *MEETINGS: The meetings of the local church are for both edification and evangelism (with no sharp distinction between these)*

5. *MINISTERS: The ministers of the local church are all its members*

6. *FOCUS: The local church should focus on doing a few things really well*

7. *SACRIFICE: The local church exists for the sake of others*

8. *PRAYER: Prayer lies at the heart of the local church*

1) BIBLE

The word of God does the work of God through the Spirit of God in the people of God

From the creation of the world ('And God said', Gen. 1:3) to the end of this present age ('with a loud command', 1 Thess. 4:16), God speaks his will into being. God the Son is called 'the Word' (John 1:1,2). God the Father, God the Son, and God the Holy Spirit use the word of God to bring about all God's purposes. That word is living and active (Heb. 4:12). The Triune God creates and shapes his people by it. It is not the people who create the word. So, although the early Christian community wrote the New Testament documents, it was the word of the gospel that had brought that community into existence in the first place.

When Simon Peter acknowledged Jesus to be 'the Christ, the Son of the living God' on the road to Caesarea Philippi (Matt. 16:16), Jesus called him the 'rock' on which he would build his church. When, six verses later, Peter denied that Jesus must suffer and die, Jesus called Peter 'Satan' (Matt. 16:23). So Peter was the 'rock' when he affirmed the gospel (that Jesus was the Son of God), but he became 'Satan' when he denied the gospel (that Jesus must suffer and die). It seems that the 'rock' was not Peter himself but the affirmation of the gospel on Peter's lips. The church is formed on and by the gospel, God's message of salvation. It is founded on Jesus Christ as preached by the apostles and prophets (Eph. 2:20).

The gospel is the message that we cannot save ourselves – neither by trying to be good nor by being religious – but that only God can save us, because he sent his son Jesus to die in our place. So through the death and resurrection of Jesus, God did for us what we could never do for ourselves: he paid the penalty for our sins. Now through his Spirit he can grant us eternal life, which is to have a relationship with him in Jesus' name (John 17:3). This is the greatest and best news our world has ever heard: that individual men and women, young and old, can be in their own relationship with the God who made the universe.

Mark Ruston preached faithfully about Jesus for three decades, and that word did the work of building up a congregation to the point where it could no longer fit in the Round Church building. The history of this particular congregation has followed that pattern for half a century. It is not a story of strategies, plans, and visions for future development. The regular teaching of the Bible has shaped the strategy through the shared leadership of the church. It is the preached word that has led the church forward. Human agency has been shaped and guided by the Spirit of God through the word of God preached weekly. Trying to respond obediently to God's word as it has been taught week by week has been the way the congregation has discovered what God plans for our future. Present obedience has been more important than blue-sky planning. One of the biggest changes that has occurred in the history of the Round Church was the move from the Holy Sepulchre (Round Church) building to the St Andrew the Great building in 1994. No individual can claim the credit for that. I went on record a few months earlier saying that I would resign if the church adopted a major building project. But through regular Bible teaching God led the leadership of the church to the point where that decision was made by an overwhelming majority in the church council.

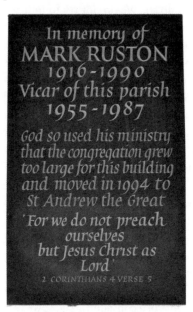

A plaque in the Round Church building celebrating Mark Ruston's thirty-two years of gospel ministry.[2]

It is my belief that change has come about through the preaching, as God has spoken through his word week by week. I did not succeed Mark Ruston with any plans to change the Round Church. I came to try to preach as faithfully as my predecessor had preached. But change happened. The word caused it to happen. No doubt we do not always hear aright, nor do we always obey what we hear. But the word of God has the power both to bring the church into existence and to direct its life.

It has been my endeavour to allow God's word to do that and not to impose human systems upon it. Neither Mark Ruston nor I were systematic theologians. But both of us were committed to teaching the word of God as faithfully as possible, and then allowing it to do its work. Therefore, we have never sought greater clarity or more precision than there is in the word of God. For example, we baptise because the word of God tells us to do so. We do not try to indicate precisely what happens at the moment of baptism, nor at what age, nor in what manner it is appropriate for it to be administered, beyond the basic guidelines of Scripture: that baptism should be with water, in the name of the Trinity and in the context of faith. Similarly, we celebrate the Lord's Supper because we are commanded to do so in the Bible, and not because we understand precisely what it signifies. Indeed, we pray because Scripture tells us to do so, not because we understand fully how prayer works.

This is not to say that we should not ponder these matters of Baptism, the Lord's Supper or prayer. But nor should we seek to achieve a clarity beyond Scripture. That way much disagreement lies, and no edification or evangelism occurs. We do not expect to get God's will exactly right. We expect the word of God to be constantly correcting us. God said through his prophet Isaiah: 'Whether you turn to the right or to the left, your ears will hear a voice behind you, saying, "This is the way; walk in it."' (Isa. 30:21). It is a mistake to think of Christian discipleship as a straight arrow. It is more of a constant zigzag, as we veer first too much in one direction and then too much in the other – just as Simon Peter needed to be affirmed when he called Jesus, 'the Christ, the Son of the living God' and rebuked when he sought to deflect him from the Cross. Such is the nature of our human state. That means we need a word from God to correct us *every* day. This is true for churches as well as for individuals. Both need a constant touch on the rudder, correcting each effort we make to obey. God's word provides that.

The word of God doing the work of God will also mean that gospel work must always be done in a gospel way. There is never room for cutting corners, or selling people short, when it comes to the gospel. We have to seek to teach the whole counsel of God, however counter-cultural that may be, and however unpopular to contemporary ears.

The greatest single conviction about the local church that characterises the Round Church at St Andrew the Great is this: that the word of God does the work of God through the Spirit of God in the people of God.

2) LOCAL CHURCH

The local church is the primary place where the Kingdom of Heaven impacts the kingdoms of this world

To return to Matthew 16, Jesus told Peter that he would build his church on that rock of gospel affirmation on the lips of his disciples. He then made it clear that this church community would be an expression of divine power on earth, able to conquer evil: 'The gates of Hades will not overcome it' (Matt. 16:18). Indeed, the church would so incarnate the gospel message of God's saving love through Jesus Christ that Jesus went on to say, 'I will give you the keys of the kingdom of heaven; whatever you bind on earth will be bound in heaven, and whatever you loose on earth will be loosed in heaven' (Matt. 16:19). What the gospel community does on earth reverberates in heaven. The rest of the New Testament is the story of small Christian communities being brought into existence by the gospel (the word of God) in different locations around the Mediterranean world (Acts 14:21–28; 15:41; 18:23; 1 Pet. 1:1–2, etc.).

The local church is not spoken of in the New Testament as a part of the universal church, but as the full local expression of the universal church in a particular place. It is 'the church of Jesus Christ at a particular place' rather than 'the little bit of the church of Jesus Christ at a particular place'. So, we need to view the local church in the light of God's calling – 'a chosen people, a royal priesthood, a holy nation, a people belonging to God, that you may declare the praises of him

"the honour of teaching a local church is enormous"

who called you out of darkness into his wonderful light' (1 Pet. 2:9). Or, in the quotation attributed to G.K. Chesterton, the church is 'rushing through the ages as the winged thunderbolt of thought and everlasting enthusiasm; a thing without rival or resemblance, and still as new as it is old'. Therefore the honour of teaching a local church is enormous. Thomas Carlyle is said to have asked, 'Who, being called to be a preacher, would stoop to be a king?' I remember Giles Walter (curate at the Round Church 1986 to 1993) asking me at the Round Church door after the evening service one Sunday, 'Can you think of anything in the world we could have better spent our time doing these last twelve hours?' I could not.

The key characteristic of both Mark Ruston's ministry and mine is that we concentrated on the all-absorbing demand of running a local church, in the belief that this is a great task – greater than climbing the structural hierarchy of the Church of England, greater than getting involved in denominational politics, more significant than speaking at conferences, or travelling the world, or even writing books about the local church! Not all Christian leaders are called to this work; God sets people apart for all sorts of different roles within the body of Christ. But the best leader of a local church will be the person who is convinced that there is no higher calling in the world and that the New Testament role of pastor-teacher in the local congregation is *the* job above all others, and who is grateful to God every day for the privilege of serving in that way. Such are the men needed to lead our local churches.

Para-church organisations (like denominations and Christian campaigning groups) are necessary to help co-ordinate Christian work in a fallen world, which is full of misunderstanding and miscommunication even among Christians. But the size and the glamour which can accompany the work of such organisations should not distract from the top priority gospel work of the local church. The size and glamour of a very large local church have some of the same dangers. After moving from the Round Church building to the St Andrew the Great building in 1994, the Round Church at St Andrew the Great took the decision not to try to go on growing in Cambridge city-centre, but rather to try to reproduce other medium-sized churches in the Cambridge area. We did not wish to become a mega-church, not just because this does not seem to be in line with New Testament practice, but more because it is not in line with New Testament principles, where God does his work through things that are weak in the eyes of the world (2 Cor. 4:7–12). Some of the consequences of this decision are described in Chapter 10.

It is because of this primacy of the local church that longevity in ministry is usually desirable. There may be a few men who are particularly gifted at leading a church through the early stages of growth, and then do best to pass the baton to someone else. But in general the best pastor-teacher will not be the one who is constantly wondering whether he should move on to new pastures or whether there is a better job on offer somewhere else. Patterns of church life which constantly move pastors from one church to another (as in the contemporary Methodist circuit) rarely build a local congregation over the years. It is characteristic of most of the strongest evangelical churches in the UK at the beginning of the twenty-first century that they have all enjoyed prolonged ministries by their main preachers. Mark Ruston served the Round Church for thirty-two years (and declined tempting offers to move elsewhere), and I have served the Round Church at St Andrew the Great for twenty-two years (and would have loved to serve longer). As time passes in a preacher's ministry, it gets harder and harder to lead purely by innovation or human energy. But it is only with time that a minister gets to know and understand his congregation, and to be known and understood by them (even the changing congregation of a student church). Only by faithfully teaching the word of God will an individual's leadership stay fresh and revitalising over decades.

The second conviction that has shaped the ministry of the Round Church at St Andrew the Great is that the local fellowship of believers is at the very centre of God's purposes for the human race.

3) EXPOSITORY PREACHING

Consecutive expository preaching by the pastor-teacher is the best normal diet of the local church

A third conviction is that the healthiest and most nourishing diet of the local church is the pastor-teacher teaching the congregation the whole counsel of God – in other words, taking them through consecutive Bible passages week by week. If God is the perfect communicator and the believer lives by every word that comes out of his mouth (Matt. 4:4), then there can be no better diet for a congregation. Human lectionaries that 'butterfly' around Scripture, flitting from one passage to another, will never feed a congregation adequately. Too many local churches, while paying lip service to the authority and sufficiency of God's word, insert the filter of the minister's own thinking and taste between the congregation and God's word when deciding on the church preaching programme. So the congregation only gets to hear from those parts of the Bible which the minister likes or thinks appropriate for his congregation.

Clearly there is a role for sanctified common sense. The wise teacher has to ponder, search out and set in order many things (Eccles. 12:9). So a planned preaching series is not inappropriate, but it must be shaped by the conviction that God is the perfect communicator and knows better than any human leader how to feed his flock. In the last resort, the word will do God's work. God does not need human agency. But he delights to use human speakers, when they are faithful to his word.

Mark Ruston habitually booked up the speakers whom the Cambridge Inter-Collegiate Christian Union (CICCU) had invited to give their Saturday night 'Bible Readings', in order to secure the ministry of the best Bible teachers in the country on a regular basis during term-time for the congregation. It was standard practice for a visiting speaker to speak for the CICCU on the Saturday night in the Cambridge Union Society building (or the large Lensfield Road Chemistry Lecture Theatre), to stay overnight with Mark Ruston in 37 Jesus Lane, to speak on the Sunday morning at the service in the Round Church, and to speak again on the Sunday evening for the CICCU's evangelistic sermon, often in Holy Trinity Church or Great St Mary's. A great many students of those days (including me) can testify to the superb grounding in Christian doctrine that such weekends provided. Having said this, my conviction was that I led St Andrew the Great most effectively by preaching regularly myself.

In practice, if a preacher is to be a true servant of God's word, he will have to give the best part of his days to studying the Bible for himself at his desk. It will mean the pain of hard and disciplined preparation, and prayer for God's help to apply the message of the passage into the realities of the society and individual lives of the hearers. The best sermons are those that have cost the preacher most, which means there needs to be an existential engagement with the word of God by the preacher through the week if the congregation is to be adequately fed on a Sunday. It will mean that from time to time the preacher needs to apologise to his congregation – perhaps because he has not worked as hard at the text as he should have done, or because he now realises that he got a previous passage wrong. He will not duck out of the harder and more challenging parts of the Bible. Of the two small Old Testament prophets concerned with the city of Nineveh, how often do we hear a series of sermons on Jonah and how rarely on Nahum? Personally, I found that preaching on the Song of Songs, Lamentations and the second half of Daniel (because they had been avoided in the preaching programme of the church for many years) proved to be a great blessing to me and, I think, to the congregation.

There is an important caveat to be made at this point: sequential exposition should be the staple diet of the local congregation, but it is not always the best way to handle the teaching programme of a youth camp or the equivalent. That may well be an appropriate place for systematic teaching where the key elements of the gospel of Christ can be taught in the limited time available. In that way the listener can grasp something of the whole plan of God in a short compass. Our minds are as weak and as sinful as the rest of our beings. And they need assistance in absorbing truth. So, the teaching programme for the youth group in a local church, or other group programmes, will not always be best served only by sequential exposition. There is an important place for 'systematic theology', which helps the human mind to comprehend and retain God's truth.

So, in general, expository preaching should be the staple diet for the local church. In his little book *The Priority of Preaching*, Christopher Ash (curate 1993 to 1997) makes the astute point that preaching is culturally neutral: 'Every culture knows what it is to sit and listen to an authoritative human being speak. That is not culturally specific. You do not need to be literate to do that.

"expository preaching should be the staple diet for the local church"

You do not need to be educated to do that. You do not need to be fluent or competent in debate to do that. Every human being can do that and that is what preaching is.'[3] He goes on, 'An interactive Bible study is not culturally-neutral. To sit around drinking coffee with a book open, reading and talking about that book in a way that forces me to keep looking at the book and finding my place and showing a high level of mental agility, functional literacy, spoken coherence and fluency, that is something only some of the human race are comfortable doing.'[4] The group Bible study, which we so value, has only been possible since the invention of the printing press, while preaching (one man addressing a group of people from God's word) has been the staple diet of the people of God from the time of the book of Deuteronomy right through to the twenty-first century. Regular expository preaching remains the staple diet for the healthy church.

Many church leaders agonise over how they can move a congregation from one condition to a better state. The answer is by preaching. Not by springing ideas, however biblical they may be, on the church council, but by feeding the flock with the word of God regularly, so that God's word pastors, leads, directs and changes both individuals and the whole body. It will move them step by step closer to his will. Such progress may not be apparent in the short term but, in the long term, faithful weekly exposition will move a congregation a long way; and through the Spirit it will create genuine change of heart and attitude in the congregation in a way that mere human leadership – however vital and inspired – can never do.

The third conviction about the local church is that its normal diet should be the sequential exposition of Scripture.

4) MEETINGS

The meetings of the local church are for edification and evangelism together (with no sharp distinction between these)

Most twenty-first century Christian believers assume that the Bible teaches us to meet together regularly in order to *worship* God. But the New Testament actually teaches that the whole life of the believer is worship (Rom. 12). As Christians we meet together, not specifically for worship, but so that we may encourage one another – in particular, to persevere in the faith and 'toward love and good deeds' (Heb. 10:23–25). Because all of life is to be a bowing down to God, our meetings ought to be characterised by corporate worship (bowing down together). But it is not as if we begin to worship when we meet and stop worshipping when we leave the meeting, any more than we start breathing when we arrive and stop breathing when we leave.

'Worship' is the concept by which we relate the whole of life to God. Whatever we do with our physical bodies is how we worship God (Rom. 12:1–2). So there is no part of life that has not become spiritual for the believer. The secular/sacred divide is removed by worship. So gatherings of Christians are not the special context for worship. And by using the term as if they were, we may re-instate an un-Biblical secular/sacred divide.

Those gatherings are for encouragement, edification (building each other up in our faith) and evangelism (see 1 Cor. 14). There is no sharp distinction to be drawn between edification and evangelism at Christian meetings. This is another distinction we love to make, thinking that a church service must *either* be aimed at building up Christians in their faith *or* at introducing non-Christians to the faith. But it is a distinction that the New Testament does not make. There, people are evangelised by being taught the truth, and they are pastored by being taught the truth. So edification and evangelism are both

> *"our meetings must be designed to bring all human beings...to encounter the living God"*

achieved by the meeting together of God's people humbly and attentively under his word. A meeting where we think the Bible passage speaks mainly to Christians ought still to contain the gospel of Jesus so that a visiting non-Christian will be evangelised. And a meeting (such as a Guest Service) aimed especially at non-Christians will bless and benefit the Christian, who also needs to be evangelised regularly.

Non-Christians frequently walk through the door of a church building. Every time they do, we must take them seriously. Church services should always be planned partly with the non-Christian visitor in mind. At one level this means introducing and leading the meeting clearly so that the newcomer is not embarrassed (when everybody around him or her seems to know what to do and he or she has not been told!). It also means that in preaching we try hard to show awareness that there will be interested non-Christians present. The inevitable interruptions that occur in the services of a city-centre church (buskers on the pavements, ambulance sirens racing past, roadwork drills) are welcome reminders of where we are and what our purpose is. Our meetings are set at the heart of the chaos that is modern life, which is not to say that there should not be moments of peace and quiet for reflection, but rather that church services must always take their context seriously. If we believe God's word will do his work, our meetings must allow that to happen. They must be designed to bring all human beings (whatever their spiritual state) to encounter the living God. The normal Sunday services of a local church can be its most effective evangelistic tool. But that means that every part of those services will have to be carefully planned with this in mind. A formal liturgy (if that is being used) must be controlled by this theological conviction: that the meetings of the local church are for edification and evangelism, as God's word does his work among his people by his Spirit.

Mark Ruston modelled his Sunday morning 'student service' at the Round Church on the type of independent school chapel service or fairly traditional Anglican morning service with which many of the undergraduates of the 1960s would have been familiar. This was not in order to appeal only to Christian students, or to just a particular social class of student. It was to pitch the service where it would have the widest familiarity among the undergraduate population of the time. A student could attend the service at the Round without any sense of encountering something unusual or strange. That allowed him or her to come under the sound of the gospel without having to deal with other unnecessary obstacles. It meant the word could do its work with a minimum of cultural interference.

The cultural and religious background has since changed beyond recognition. In the twenty-first century there is no equivalent model for our services, but we still seek to uphold the same principle of allowing the word to do the work without cultural hindrances. Therefore, we reckon that a service of about an hour's length is the appropriate duration in our particular (and in many ways unusual) culture. That allows Christian members of the congregation to invite their non-Christian friends with complete confidence that the service will end pretty well exactly an hour after it has begun. The young families particularly appreciate consistent control of the length of services, for the sake of their children, and any other families they may wish to invite. Christian congregation members might well prefer a longer service, but they need to be constantly reminded that church services are not for them alone.

This may mean restricting the usual length of the sermon for cultural reasons. It is a mistake to think that preaching is necessarily better for being longer. Most preachers preach less well for being allowed to preach as long as they like. A church that values preaching will endeavour to bring the best out of its preachers, and providing them with time guidelines is one way to do that. In Cambridge we have the privilege of hearing many great visiting preachers. It is easy to spot those who are not getting regular critical feedback on their sermons and are ill-disciplined about timing. John Stott became our model for always preaching exactly to the time that was suggested.

In order to avoid unnecessary barriers, we need to remove any possible cause of embarrassment from a service. We need to keep asking, 'Will doing this in this way in the service make someone feel uncomfortable?' And nothing has greater potential for embarrassment than music. Community singing is not a common activity in our culture now. Moreover there is a huge diversity of musical taste. It will not be possible to pick songs which please the taste of everyone present. So we have to select a position at some approximate cultural mid-way point for the sort of congregation attending the church service (and, at the Round Church at St Andrew the Great, the age demographic would be below thirty years old), and then try to do what we do with our music as best we can. Even though an item in a service may not suit my taste, the better it is done the less uncomfortable I will feel about it.

The pursuit of excellence communicates to the visitor that we are in earnest. The world will think us weak and unimpressive, but we need to show them that we think it matters and we are doing our best. There should be nothing shoddy about the way we do things. There should be no doubt of the seriousness of what we are about, nor of its accessibility. The outsider may not agree with the Christian faith, but he or she must be able to see that it matters a very great deal to us, and that we are communicating about it in terms that are intelligible to him or to her. It will be strange for a non-Christian in the twenty-first century to attend a gathering in which a fairly large number of his or her contemporaries are giving serious attention to a religious text two thousand or more years old. But we want them to feel as comfortable as possible in starting to listen closely to that text for themselves. It is helpful in every service to let the non-Christians present know that they are expected and welcome. A courteous and unembarrassing 'opt-out' or excuse not to join in with inappropriate parts of the service (like a Creed or a devotional song) can be given by saying something like, 'Not all of us will be able to say or sing these words'; and we try to answer within the first few sentences of any sermon the question in the mind of any bored non-believer present: 'why should I go on listening to this preacher for one more minute?' We try never to assume that only Christians are present (except at the monthly mid-week prayer meetings). We do not want the non-Christian to feel like an interloper, eavesdropping on a meeting of an esoteric sect, but rather to be reassured that it is all right to be present as a welcome guest who has not yet decided about Jesus Christ for himself or herself.

Because we are serious about what we are doing in our services, we can never take lightly the words we sing. Voltaire once said: 'If a thing is too silly to be said, it can always be sung', and we know the truth of that in the lyrics of some Christian songs. There are many popular contemporary Christian songs which we find we are unable to sing at the Round Church at St Andrew the Great simply because the words are unhelpful or doctrinally wrong. There are other songs where we have suggested changes in the lyrics to the author, and occasionally we have received their blessing to make that change. There is no doubt that congregation members remember the words they sing. It can be one of the most helpful ways of memorising Scripture. But singing is a dangerously powerful tool, and we need to be constantly alert as to whether it is building or undermining the faith of the congregation, and pointing the non-Christian faithfully to Christ.

Our fourth conviction is that the local church meets in order to hear God's word, which will edify the believer and evangelise the non-believer.

5) MINISTERS

The ministers of the local church are all its members

The teaching of the Bible is not the leader's preserve. It is the task of the whole congregation. It is not confined to the pulpit. It actually goes on at every level of the church's life. While some individuals are paid to organise the church's life and to be free to teach the Bible publicly throughout the week, all Christians are ministers of the gospel. It is the privilege and responsibility of every Christian to teach others about God, and to live and work in the world for God. There are no more important tasks.

It will not help church members to think that the church is led by the people who take decisions on committees; so that the most important task a member can fulfil is to serve on one of those committees. 'How important am I compared with others?' is always an illegitimate question in the life of the local church. If the church is led by the word of God, then those who teach the word (in any form) are leading the church. Attending meetings, organising the church's life, or taking decisions are not at the top of a hierarchy of ministry. In fact there is no hierarchy of ministry and, if there were, such things would come low down the list.

As the Bible is taught in the congregation (with people then teaching each other), it will inevitably drive the individual members of that congregation out into the world to serve God in whatever he calls them to. All church members must be encouraged to think how they can serve God for themselves in the world.

There will be many different roles for them to play, and the rest of the congregation will not necessarily own those same roles or ministries. The Round Church at St Andrew the Great over the years has resisted pressure from individual members to adopt all the different ministries its members have been involved in. As a bachelor, Mark Ruston recognised that he had limited capability for children's, youth and family ministry. He focused on what he could do well (teach the Bible and minister to students) while allowing other congregation members to develop other aspects of the church's mission.

So we try to draw a notional boundary around what we concentrate our collective energy upon. It is the boundary of Bible teaching. We focus the church's resources on that, in the recognition that the Bible faithfully taught will then drive the church's members out into the world in all forms of Christian service and evangelism.

This is a generalisation in the life of the Round Church at St Andrew the Great, rather than a hard and fast rule. There are notable exceptions – like Bounce-A-Round, the large parents, carers and toddlers group which meets on a Wednesday. This is an example to the congregation of engagement with the world outside the church: it provides a service to the community, resourced by Christians, and is intended to provide a natural way for non-Christians to encounter Christ. In the same way, we have a small working group which addresses the issues of homelessness in central Cambridge on behalf of, and with the help of, the rest of the congregation.

But it is very easy for Christian social involvement to take on a life of its own, so that it can come to dominate the life of a local church, resulting in the church gradually losing its own gospel heart and gospel purpose. Only when a local church understands that its primary task is to teach the Bible faithfully to its members will those members be guarded against distracting and diluting tendencies in their world involvement. They must be involved in the world, but they must remain centred on the gospel. Only Bible teaching can achieve that.

This is not to say that within the local church we do things together but, in the wider world, work alone as individuals. The nature of the Christian life is corporate and we always do things together as Christians, if possible. The normal word for a Christian believer in the New Testament ('saint') comes sixty-one times in the plural out of its sixty-two occurrences (and even the sixty-second occurrence, Philippians 4:21, is in a plural sense!).[5] The strong cult of the individual, which has arisen in Western society since the Renaissance and which gives us such a strong concern for privacy and confidentiality, has little to do with the Christianity of the New Testament. There we are encouraged to invest heavily in one another's lives, to work together for God's kingdom on earth. And so we must. But this does not mean that every local church should

"the ministers of the local church are all its converted members"

adopt everything that each one of its members gets involved in. One fatal temptation for the local church is to take on too much. If we believe the word of God does the work of God, we can trust it to equip the

people of God to do what God wants done in his world. The local church leadership must concentrate on the primary task of the local church – teaching the Bible faithfully to the congregation – while empowering and equipping the congregation members to be ministers of the gospel in many different spheres and ways.

So, in order to free the members to serve God as he calls them to, we have found it necessary to limit the activities of the Round Church at St Andrew the Great. Meetings are restricted to certain nights of the week so that church activities do not invade the entire lives of church members. (Committees meet on Mondays, Bible study groups on Wednesdays, aiming to leave other evenings free.) As a congregation we very rarely advertise other Christian causes, not because we do not approve of them, but to lower the pressure on each other's lives. Local churches can run on guilt; but just as grace, not merit, is the heart of our theology, so gratitude, not guilt, should be the heart of our ethics (our Christian behaviour). It is always a battle to restrain the 'internal temperature' of a church. It is always easier to start new meetings in church life than to stop ones that have passed their 'sell-by' date. If all the members of the congregation are its ministers, they must not have their lives so full of 'church' activity that they do not have the time or energy to be effective servants of the gospel in the world. It is the task of the paid church staff to free them up for that.

Our fifth conviction is that the ministers of the local church are all its converted members. They meet week by week to be taught the Bible to equip them for their many ministries.

6) FOCUS

The local church should focus on doing a few things really well

We have already discussed the priority of Bible teaching and the danger of dissipating the church's energies by adopting too many programmes and ministries. Most local churches can do only a few things really well. To teach the Bible properly will require a lot of the church's resources to be dedicated to that end. But this principle of focus will have other consequences in the life of the church as well.

Being located in the centre of a city with a number of other churches meeting only a few metres away has meant that the Round Church at St Andrew the Great has been able to concentrate on faithful Bible teaching without coming under intolerable pressure to be all things to all people. Mark Ruston maintained a very clear direction for thirty-two years which meant that he passed a very united church on to me. If a church is like a bus (as John Wimber once remarked), displaying its intended destination clearly for all to see, then thirty-two years is a long enough time for the passengers to get absolutely clear that this is the bus they want to be on, rather than one which is going somewhere else. Many church leaders, in an attempt to please as many people as possible, have their churches displaying a confused message about their destination, which causes frustration and false expectations among the membership. So one result of a clear focus at the Round/St Andrew the Great has been a united congregation.

Mark Ruston also recognised his own limitations as a church leader and learnt to play to his strengths. With a background in independent schools and in school and college chaplaincy, he had a special gift for dealing with students one-to-one. He was an expert 'personal worker'. Such ministry is intensive. A lot of time and energy is poured into just a few people. Mark Ruston had carefully chosen students to lodge with him at 37 Jesus Lane because he knew the value of dealing in depth with a few in order to reach the many.

It is striking how narrowly Jesus focused his ministry. He concentrated on the Jews largely to the exclusion of Gentiles. He used parables to sift out from among his casual listeners those with a genuine interest (Mark 4:11). From his serious followers, he picked seventy to send out; but from within the seventy he had a prior commitment to twelve; and even within the twelve he chose three to accompany him at a number of key moments in his ministry: the raising of Jairus' daughter, the transfiguration, Gethsemane. Even within those three Jesus singled out Peter for special attention (and

"there was a clear focus to Jesus' ministry"

perhaps also 'the disciple whom Jesus loved', John, the author of the fourth Gospel). Undoubtedly, Jesus could have influenced more people – many more were eager to come within his orbit – but there was a clear focus to his ministry. He worked outwards from strength, building up one or two of a small inner group, and then the twelve, and, from that unlikely beginning, founding the church that has spread throughout the world. No single life has been as effective as his in impacting the whole human race.

Mark Ruston showed the Round Church at St Andrew the Great the value of investing deeply in the lives of a few other people. 'Personal work' is a feature of the church's ministry. We try to provide the most faithful Bible teaching we can from the pulpit. We try to ensure that the Bible is at the heart of the programmes for the children, youth, students, young adults, home groups, internationals and senior members. We help members to set up prayer triplets, where three friends meet regularly to share needs and pray for one another. But we particularly encourage two Christians (often an older and a younger) to get together with an open Bible to discuss and apply God's word. All the church's staff members are expected to be a part of this. It is in such meetings that much of the most effective discipling of the church goes on. When two people are looking at the Bible it is much less easy to fall into the trap of applying its truths to others rather than myself; it is natural to ask questions if I cannot understand a passage; I can get to grips with God's word and, more importantly, it can get to grips with me. And I often form a profound and life-changing relationship with another person in the process.

Even within this focus on 'personal work', there needs to be a focus on the simple truths of the gospel. I was converted on 7 February 1968 when, after vociferous arguments with undergraduate friends, I was introduced by these friends to Jonathan Fletcher who, instead of answering all my arguments, sat me down and explained the gospel to me. He showed me that I needed to *Admit* that I was a sinner (Rom. 3:23; 6:23), that I needed to *Believe* that Jesus had died in my place to deal with my sin (John 3:16; Isa. 53:6); and I needed to *Come* to him (Rev. 3:20). Without that simple explanation and challenge to respond, I had found it impossible to get a handle on Christianity.

At the heart of all personal work lies a simple gospel explanation. It may sometimes be too early in the life of a particular person to go over the gospel in such simple terms, but it is never too late. The gospel lies at the very heart of the Christian life and we never grow out of it or go beyond it. Every step forward in our discipleship is always also a step back to the foot of the cross. 'Personal work' focuses above all else on those simple truths; and it is in the light of them that a huge range of other topics can be tackled when we meet one-to-one. Mark Ruston brought many students to Christ with such a simple focus.

The gospel calls us to change – the change of conversion if we are not yet Christian, and the change of sanctification (growing more like Jesus) if we are. But, individually, we find it very hard to change ourselves. We need the help of a community – exhorting, challenging, rebuking, encouraging one another – which is why the church must always be a change-enabling community. And the most effective way the community helps me to change is one-to-one. Only there can I find the security to acknowledge my particular weaknesses, failures and sins and, with the help of one other person, confront and conquer them.

So there has been over the years a focus on personal work in the Round Church at St Andrew the Great, encouraging the members to speak personally to their friends, both to share the gospel in evangelism and to study it in discipleship. Personal work is one of the scarcely seen ways that God's word does his work in his world. It is an example of the value of focusing ministry, not on what the world approves and applauds, but on what God intends and purposes.

After twenty years of ministry in Cambridge I approached my churchwardens to ask whether they would consider freeing me up for a wider role in the church at large, a bit like a 'Rector emeritus'. I felt that I had focused within Cambridge quite narrowly for two decades, and it might now be appropriate to play a rather different role, while the very strong staff team handled the day-to-day running of St Andrew the Great. The churchwardens, under John Anstead's leadership, asked for time without me present to ponder the question and then in effect replied, 'No'! It was a little more nuanced than that – the exact words of their memo were:

> *In principle, the wardens are in agreement that you should be able to do more work away from St Andrew the Great. However, we believe that God has called you to serve him as our main Bible teacher and leader of our congregation and that this should continue to be your principal area of service. We feel that this is vital, not only for the lay congregation, but also for our paid staff and those who are considering full-time Christian work. We would still expect to see you present and active, either preaching or leading, at the majority of services.* (Email from John Anstead to Mark Ashton, 6 June 2007)

After initial disappointment, I realised just how affirming such a reply was. The team of four churchwardens was absolutely clear that I was doing what God intended me to do, and I could not be more profitably engaged in the service of the kingdom anywhere else. So I withdrew my request.

That affirmed for me the value of focus in the local church – that the cost of doing the most important things of all as best we can will always entail neglecting other good and worthy things. We need to learn to distinguish what really matters from what matters, but matters less. One missionary used to have a plaque on his desk that read 'Planned Neglect' to remind himself of just this point. At Christopher Ash's suggestion, I had over my desk the words of the Puritan divine, William Perkins (who preached in the St Andrew the Great building at the end of the sixteenth century) – 'Thou art a minister of the Word; Mind thy Business!' (Christopher Ash named his golden retriever 'Perkins', which seemed less useful!). C.J. Davis (curate 1994 to 2000) once helpfully clarified the aim of the Marriage Preparation ministry at St Andrew the Great by saying, 'We are not trying to prevent people divorcing: we are trying to get people to heaven.' In other words, the team members were not pretending to be marriage counsellors or sex therapists; they were teaching the Bible to engaged couples as the surest way of guarding their future marriages. We needed to keep our eye on the ultimate goal in order to achieve the intermediate goal of healthy Christian marriages.

Focus in the local church will mean ignoring many of the things that the world expects us to do (the things that often bring the most glory and honour in the world's eyes) in order to channel our resources into the (often less glamorous) tasks God calls us to.

7) SACRIFICE

The local church exists for the sake of others

Archbishop William Temple perceptively remarked that 'The church is the only co-operative society in the world which exists for the benefit of its non-members.' Self-sacrifice is a hallmark of healthy church life.

The pattern established by Jesus himself (Phil. 2:4–11) is one of self-humbling. But it is not just humiliation for its own sake. Isaiah 53 teaches us that the pain of substitution is balanced by the blessing it brings to others: 'But he was pierced for our transgressions, he was crushed for our iniquities; the punishment that brought us peace was upon him, and by his wounds we are healed' (Isa. 53:5). 'Taking the pain so that others may get the blessing' is the biblical pattern for the individual Christian life and for the life of local churches.

Mark Ruston taught the adult congregation to serve the student community in the centre of Cambridge. 'Town' members of the congregation quickly learned that the church had a mission to undergraduate students which was costly and inconvenient. The

Sunday morning family service would change its meeting time six times a year, as it was moved forward in term-time to make room for the later student service, and then reverted out-of-term to a more convenient, mid-morning time. Changing service times is thoroughly uncomfortable for families and non-student members of the congregation and, at every change, some forget and arrive embarrassingly early or embarrassingly late. No text book on *How to Grow a Successful Church* would ever advocate such a tactic. But there must be few more eloquent reminders to a congregation that they do not exist for their own convenience.

When I started as vicar of the Round Church in 1987, I was advised by an experienced leader of a large student church in another country to aim to wrap up the work of the university Christian Union in my first couple of years. Adults can minister to students much more effectively than students can minister to one another, and a student work resourced and staffed by a local church will, in human terms, 'outcompete' a student work run by students for students. But I followed the pattern I had inherited – that the Round Church served the student work of the Cambridge Inter-Collegiate Christian Union and did not try to dominate it, and that has remained our endeavour. God has delighted to use the weakness of student leadership to his own glory, as God always delights to use human weakness (1 Cor. 1).[6] Another senior church leader of a student church provided another, more pragmatic, rationale for supporting student leadership in student work: 'If the CICCU goes off the rails theologically,' he said, 'it can be back on again in a year or two. But if a local church goes the same way, it can take decades to restore it.' So if we allow student work to be dominated by local churches, the potential for harm is very great.

At the end of the 1980s, the Round Church Parochial Church Council, after various revisions, agreed a 'Vision Statement' which tried to encapsulate the church's conviction. One of its three main statements reads: 'A church committed to a specific mission: it is our special task to serve the university communities in which we are placed. There are two aspects to the work of our church ('town and gown'), but both depend on one another: by becoming a better 'normal' church, we also become a better student church.'

All healthy churches need to have a mission for which they sacrifice themselves, and a focus for that mission in some 'target' group. During his ministry at Eden Baptist Church in Cambridge, Roy Clements wrote:

> *Do you want to know how to kill a church? Fasten its members' attention purely on internal matters. Get them agitated about what hymnbook they should sing from. Make them anxious about charismatic enthusiasm in their midst, or about the sins of the ecumenical movement. Get them totally absorbed in a new building programme, or in fund-raising activities, or in simply being nosey about one another's problems. It does not really matter what the issue is, so long as it has the effect of drying up their outreach. Then stand back and wait for spiritual gangrene to set in and do its lethal work. Go back a generation or two later and you will find that church has become one of those nasty cliques that are dominated by a handful of inter-bred families who cannot give up the habit of church-going. The church will have been murdered. To be more precise, it will have committed suicide. If such a church remains orthodox, it is a dead orthodoxy; if it retains a congregation, it is a lifeless congregation. As often as not, of course, they do neither. They simply disappear, leaving their once busy churches to be turned into factories or mosques.*

A young family joined the Round Church early in my ministry and after a year the father complained to me that he had come to realise that any money he gave to the Round Church would not be spent on a youth worker to look after his two teenage children, but on student workers to care for the students. He announced that the family was leaving for another Cambridge church with better youth and children's provision. I felt deeply apologetic that we had not made that clear to the family from the outset. We are a church that sacrifices our own interests for the sake of a mission to students.

But this culture of self-sacrifice has been a constant spiritual tonic to the vitality of the congregation. Just as long-term consistency in the ministry has united the congregation over the decades, so an attitude of self-sacrifice has kept the congregation gospel-hearted. It has sieved out from the congregation those for whom church attendance is primarily a matter of meeting their own needs, and which is to be done at their own convenience. The final sentences of that vision statement read: 'We believe that God means us to grow, individually and as a church; that growth is change; and that change may be painful. We accept the pain of change gladly for the sake of bringing the gospel to our contemporaries'. Accepting the pain of change gladly is much easier to say than to do, but in the pain of change we have discovered so much of God's blessing.

Trevor Huddleston once wrote a book with a most striking title – *Naught for your Comfort* – which seems a very good motto for local church life. It has been wisely said that spiritually healthy churches lurch from one financial crisis to another. That dictum has been a comfort to many church treasurers, and one long-term member of the congregation at the Round Church at St Andrew the Great said that, in his opinion, the only time when he had been

"the gospel is never about seeking our own comfort"

aware that the church was slightly stagnant spiritually coincided with a time of no financial worry. The gospel is never about seeking our own comfort, and it always drives the local church out to do more for God in the world.

After the completion of the rebuilding work on St Andrew the Great in 1994, the church leadership was not minded to expand the building's capacity in order to grow the church in that way any further. Instead we were moved by the Bible teaching to a conviction that we should seek to plant or graft a part of the congregation into other local church situations where the ministry was weaker. Consequently in 1997 Christopher and Carolyn Ash took forty adults and children to All Saints, Little Shelford (a village five miles to the south); then, in 2004, Steve and Beth Midgley took over 100 adults and children to Christ Church (a mile to the north east); and in 2008 Frank and Katherine Price took a similar number to St Matthew's (a mile to the east).

Each of these church plant leaders first joined the staff team at St Andrew the Great with the encouragement to preach so well that in a few years a good number of the congregation would happily leave St Andrew the Great with them to reinforce the life of another church. Fundamental to that model of church-planting is not just that it is a gifted Bible teacher or just a group of congregation members, but the two together: a Bible teacher with a group who want to be taught the Bible by that teacher.

When preparing for one of these church plants, any and all members of the congregation have been encouraged to sign up for it. There has been no selection process by the church staff. No-one has been ordered to go or forbidden to go. There has always been a period of prayer and preparation; particularly as such Church Growth Initiatives are peculiarly hazardous and problematic within Anglican structures even with the support of the Diocesan Bishop. Then, when the moment has come, the 'umbilical cord' has been cut at once – all financial giving transferred and everyone encouraged to make a clean break from the parent congregation. Each of the church leaders involved has been faced with a sink-or-swim situation; but, in view of the very tough first two years which Christopher and Carolyn Ash weathered in Little Shelford, we have since always tried to ensure that there was one other full-time staff member to support the church leader. All three of the men who have done this showed immense patience and supernatural wisdom and discernment. Grafting one body of believers on to another is hugely problematic. It is greatly to their credit how well all three churches flourish.

So the Round Church at St Andrew the Great has tried to be characterised by a generosity to other Christian work. We only give away approximately ten percent of our financial income to support other Christian work at home and overseas (knowing that there are many churches which are more generous than that), but we have tried to conduct our church life in a self-sacrificial way – giving away about a third of our student members every year, giving away a much higher proportion of the normal church congregation on a regular basis in church plants, and glad to accept the pain of that for the sake of others. We are convinced that self-sacrifice is essential in the local church.

8) PRAYER

Prayer lies at the heart of the local church

A final conviction that has shaped the life of the Round Church at St Andrew the Great is that prayer must lie at the very heart of the local church.

Mark Ruston's quiet godliness spoke of someone who prayed a lot. In his teaching there was always a firm insistence on the 'Quiet Time' – that every Christian should try to find a time to be alone with God every day. On their wedding day Mark Ruston would give couples a copy of *Step by Step* by John Eddison to take away on their honeymoon with them, so that they started married life together with the Bible and prayer at its centre.[7]

Prayer and Bible reading have to go together. The way the Bible works in the life of a believer is a mystery. It is not simply an authoritative text like the Koran. Frequently it compares itself to food, so that the spiritual life of the believer is maintained by God's word ('Man does not live on bread alone, but on every word that comes from the mouth of God', Matt. 4:4). That is a dynamic image, where the believer has a part to play (eating and digesting the word). We do that by reading *and* praying over the word of God. So prayer is vital to Bible reading. In Deuteronomy 29:29, Moses told the people of Israel: 'The secret things belong to the Lord our God, but the things revealed belong to us and to our children forever, that we may follow all the words of this law.' Scripture is not a complete revelation of everything a human being might want to know. There are secret things which belong to God. But it is a dynamic revelation, revealing what we need to know in order to live God's way on earth. It interacts with my life to teach me how to live. And that happens through reading *and* praying. Every day I need to hear that voice behind me saying: 'This the way; walk in it' (Isa. 30:21), and I need to respond to it in prayerful obedience.

Prayer is how we engage with God's word, and how it engages with us. It is the place where God's Spirit gets to grips with our spirits to bring us into line with his will: 'In the same way, the Spirit helps us in our weakness. We do not know what we ought to pray for, but the Spirit himself intercedes for us with groans that words cannot express. And he who searches our hearts knows the mind of the Spirit because the Spirit intercedes for the saints in accordance with God's will' (Rom. 8:26–27). It is a mysterious and largely invisible process. It is how we participate

> *"Prayer is the place where God's Spirit gets to grips with our spirits"*

in the eternal spiritual realm, how we walk by faith and not by sight (2 Cor. 5:7). What God is doing is not easily visible to human eyes, so not all visible growth in a church will necessarily be his work. Our criterion for judging any strategy for the church must be its faithfulness to what he has said to us in the Bible, not whether it adds to our numbers. Church growth methods and 'church leadership by statistical analysis' must be judged by this criterion. *We* do not grow the church or build the congregation, and, while we think we can, we probably get in the way of the only one who actually can.

But as it is Christ's intention to build his church, then we can pray that he will do so. And prayer is exactly the right attitude to the growth of the church. We cannot have a five-year plan for it, as though we can achieve it ourselves. It is not a human achievement. But we can pray for it, as God has made his will clear in the matter. And then we can expect it, as we expect answers to all our prayers, trusting God to act in his own way and in his own time, for our best interests. There is an important distinction between seeing church growth as something we achieve by 'getting things right' (by our own clear thinking and our hard work), and seeing church growth as something God grants as and when he chooses. When we are told that we should 'plan for growth', we can alter two letters and '*pray* for growth'. Our guideline for the future development of our churches should not be 'How can I increase the size of this church?' but 'How can I bring this church more into line with the will of God so that he can fulfil his purposes for her?' The answer is by attending to the Bible and by prayer.

Change in the local church always begins in the heart of its pastor. The pastor himself must be a person who is living under the reproving, correcting, exhorting word of God and responding to it in his prayer life. If the pastor does not change (and be seen to change in ways that are costly to him personally), he should not expect his church to change. For that he will need a vibrant prayer life. He will need a reserve of energy in order to pastor a changing church. Change is emotionally expensive for all concerned. So a church leader must take time to pray.

As well as the emphasis Mark Ruston always put on the 'Quiet Time' (for himself and for others), he also insisted on the importance of the church prayer meeting. A biblical church will always be a praying church. But finding an appropriate pattern for the corporate prayer life of a local church is a tricky business. Few things engender guilt as easily as our lack of prayer. 'Does this church pray enough?' is an entirely unhelpful question in the life of a local church (along with, 'Does this church care enough?'). The answer must always be 'no'! The prayer life of a church cannot be judged by mere quantity and it is never helped by guilt.

The recent pattern at St Andrew the Great has been to cancel all the Bible study groups on the first Wednesday of each month and assemble all who can come for a monthly Church Prayer Meeting. It has become a key meeting in the life of the church (if not *the* key meeting). It is the one gathering at which we make the assumption that everyone present is a believer – although even then we apologise publicly that we are making that assumption for the sake of any outsiders present. We start with a song, a prayer of confession and a Bible exposition; and then we break into smaller groups (of six to eight) for prayer, interspersed with slots of information to fuel our praying, and songs. It lasts an hour and a half. There never seems to be anything very special about the format of the meeting. But it is undoubtedly the very heartbeat of the church.

One subsidiary but important function of the Prayer Meeting is disseminating information and sharing, because it informs the prayer life of the church for the rest of the month, along with the monthly Church Prayer Diary – the latter is a key discipling tool in the life of the congregation, as it teaches us and encourages us to pray. A church council member once said, 'If you miss the Church Prayer Meeting, you miss the news about what is going on in the life of the congregation.' It is the central hub, the heart of the church. The attendance and the atmosphere at the Church Prayer Meeting seem to provide

"The monthly Church Prayer Meeting...is undoutedly the very heartbeat of the church"

an accurate barometer for the spiritual health of the congregation (in so far as such things can ever be accurately discerned by human beings). It is the group to which the church staff and churchwardens and church council first bring new ideas, suggestions or developments so that they are first prayed over by the church before they are decided upon.

I became more and more aware during my ministry how much I owed to the prayers of the church. I found the Round Church at St Andrew the Great a wonderfully easy church to lead, partly because of the unity within the church and the gospel-heartedness of the church which I inherited from Mark Ruston, and partly because

Mark Ruston taught the church to pray – privately and together. Although the particular individuals changed over the years, the culture of the church had become deeply biblical and prayerful. That is a wonderful heritage.

Endnotes

1. In a short booklet, *On My Way to Heaven*, Mark Ashton describes his own experience of facing imminent death from inoperable cancer. Real confidence, he explains, is found in the resurrection of Jesus Christ – an event which, even though it happened 2,000 years ago, has profound implications for us today. The booklet is full of hope and ideal to give away to others. ISBN 978-1-90617-308-1. It can be obtained from www.10ofthose.com or www.amazon.co.uk.

2. Carved by Andrew Tanser BA ARBS of Guilden Morden, Herts

3. Ash, Christopher, *The Priority of Preaching*, Christian Focus Publications, 2009.

4. Ibid., pp. 27–28.

5. Based on the New International Version (1984). Other translations render the Greek as 'holy ones' or 'the Lord's people'.

6. Barclay, Oliver R., *Whatever happened to the Jesus Lane lot?* Inter-Varsity Press, 1977.

7. John Eddison's *Step by Step* is a brilliant aid to a daily 'Quiet Time' with selected Bible verses, a short comment and a very brief prayer for each day of the year. It has recently been reprinted by Authentic, ISBN 978-1-85078-819-5.

PART 2

THE STORY OF THE ROUND CHURCH (1955 TO 1994)

Two former curates and some long-standing members of the congregation give an account of the ministries of Mark Ruston and Mark Ashton during the period when the church family's home was the famous Round Church building in Cambridge. It is not a comprehensive and detailed account – rather a glimpse into what God was doing in and through these two remarkable men at that time.

CHAPTER 2

The early years (1955 to 1965)

Gordon Bridger

The parish which encircles the famous 'Church of the Holy Sepulchre' is tiny. When I became Mark Ruston's first full-time curate, I visited the whole parish with a small team in one evening! But the strategic importance of the church was obvious. It was set in the very heart of the university.

I have little first-hand experience of the ministry of Mr Potter, who preceded Mark Ruston. When I was training for ordination at Ridley Hall, I was invited to preach to the small, elderly congregation. My impression was that the small, devout group of worshippers who met regularly each Sunday had little understanding of the mission field on their doorstep. It needed someone like Mark Ruston to give to the local congregation a vision for reaching out to the university as well as the city.

Mark Ruston served his first curacy in Woking before becoming school chaplain at Cheltenham College in 1942. In 1951, he became chaplain of Jesus College, Cambridge, followed by a chaplaincy at Emmanuel College.[1] Mark's sense of call to serve in Cambridge prompted him to take a curacy at St Paul's Church hoping that, in the providence of God, a more permanent position in Cambridge would open up for him. The opportunity arose in 1955 and Mark was appointed vicar of the Round Church where he remained for the rest of his life.

Mark Ruston (right) inspecting repairs to the roof of the Round Church.[2]

I joined Mark Ruston as his first full-time curate in January 1960. After five years of Mark's faithful ministry, the Round Church was often full of students on Sunday mornings during term-time. A 'Children's Church' had been started, meeting before the main 11 o'clock service. Mark had persuaded Noel Pollard, who was studying for a PhD at Tyndale House, Cambridge, to act as a part-time curate with particular responsibility for the Children's Church (along with Mary Antcliffe and other lay leaders). A work among other young people (15–21 year-olds) began, as did an after-church fellowship in the evening (the *Stir-up Club*) led by Peter and Priscilla Hutchison.

Mark gave me two main tasks: 1) to build up the families that were beginning to come in greater numbers to the Children's Church; and 2) to support Christian students with Bible teaching and personal work, and to see the university as well as the city ('town and gown') as a mission field. It was a tall order – and a great privilege.

There was something wonderfully simple (not simplistic) and straightforward about Mark Ruston's ministry. He refused to be sidetracked by ecclesiastical politics, though much respected by the city of Cambridge and the Diocese of Ely. Indeed, he later became

Rural Dean of Cambridge, Examining Chaplain for the Bishop of Ely, Honorary Canon of Ely Cathedral, and Chaplain to Her Majesty the Queen. But none of these honours took him away from his ministry in Cambridge and his focus on three essential aspects of his ministry: prayer, preaching and people.

Prayer

In his book on the 1859 Revival in Ireland, J.T. Carson sums up the importance of prayer with the simple words: 'Things happen when we pray which do not happen when we do not pray.' Mark clearly believed that. We prayed together. We prayed with some of the church family at the weekly prayer meeting. Prayer was clearly Mark's priority.

Much of Mark's prayer life was necessarily in private (see Matt. 6:6). But it was occasionally possible to glimpse something of his diligence in prayer. Priscilla Hutchison, mentioned earlier, told me Mark prayed regularly for her family – especially for her son John, who went to America and, for a time, reacted against the faith of his parents. Mark wrote regularly to John and prayed for him persistently. After a time, John came to Christ and served as a youth leader in Liverpool. There must be numerous examples of that kind of persevering prayer. Many of us owe more than we know to being on Mark's prayer list and to being the subject of his faithful persevering prayer.

Preaching

Preaching was also at the heart of Mark's ministry. His conviction was that preaching the word of God in the presence of the people of God in the context of the worship of God was the key to people coming to faith in Christ and being built up into mature disciples – a conviction (along with the priority of prayer and people) that Mark Ashton would later share.

The services at the Round in the 1960s were very different from today's more informal style. The 1662 Prayer Book was the authorised liturgy for the Church of England. Many of the students, most of whom came from public schools, found the simple and relaxed yet dignified way in which Mark led the services was not wholly removed from their experience of school chapel. The difference for most of them was the clear biblical expository preaching they received from Mark and from visiting preachers. Each week during term, Cambridge Inter-Collegiate Christian Union (CICCU) would hold a Bible teaching meeting and an evangelistic meeting. More often than not, Mark would invite the visiting speaker to preach at the Round on the Sunday morning.

I had the joy of meeting my wife, Elizabeth, when she was a student at Girton College and I was a curate at the Round. She tells me that Mark was a favourite preacher at Girton Chapel among the teaching staff as well as the students. They appreciated his genuineness and his straightforward, practical teaching. 'It was a refreshing change from those visiting preachers who tried to preach a very academic sermon for "blue stockings"', she says!

Mark's commitment to preaching the word of God was also a motivation in setting up the 'Islington Week'[3], which was offered to students considering ordained ministry in the Church of England. I believe the idea came from Maurice Wood (then Vicar of Islington) and Mark Ruston in Cambridge. The students experienced parish life in Islington and, certainly in the early days, they had the privilege of hearing morning 'Bible Readings' from Alan Stibbs, Vice-Principal of Oak Hill Theological College and a renowned expositor. Islington weeks continued for several years and were used by God to help many to discern his calling. They also encouraged many to seek to 'preach the word' in the same faithful way that Mark (and Alan Stibbs) modelled.

People

As well as being focused on prayer and preaching, Mark's ministry was also characterised by a genuine love for people. Many valued his personal friendship, his pastoral care and his gift of clarity in explaining how to find a personal faith in Christ. This was by no means limited to students, though there must be many students who met with the living Christ through Mark's sensitive and loving witness. To name but one, a senior member of the university who was lecturer in Italian in 1957, gladly acknowledges the part Mark played in her own journey of faith. She is the distinguished scholar and writer, Dr Barbara Reynolds, and her account can be read at the end of the chapter.

Mark was a much loved pastor. As he focused on prayer, preaching and people, the work grew steadily. Perhaps the most obvious growth was among students in term-time when the church was not only regularly full but, from time to time, overflowed into the church hall on the other side of Round Church Street. Children's Church also expanded. Having started in a side aisle, the families began to fill the centre of the church as well. A Pathfinder Bible class was started for teenagers and a work among the 18–30s began to develop. All was set for a further period of growth with the appointment of David Watson as my successor in 1962. I did not know David very well but, given the impact of his later ministry and his part in what was to become the charismatic movement, it may be of interest to focus briefly on his curacy at the Round.

David came to the Round Church following a three-year curacy among the dock-workers in Gillingham, Kent.[4] In his autobiography, *You Are My God*, David wrote warmly about Mark: 'Mark Ruston... could not have been more thoughtful and caring, and his steady and faithful ministry for Christ has been one of the outstanding features in Cambridge for over twenty-seven years.'[5] After Gillingham, David found Cambridge itself something of a culture shock and 'remarkably dull'. He soon became fascinated by the great histories of revival and the outpourings of God's Spirit and, before long, he had many new experiences.[6] A little later, David told a few friends in strict confidence that he had started to speak in tongues in private prayer. This news somehow reached the biblical research centre where he was living and David was asked to leave and find other accommodation. It is not within the scope of this book to discuss the rights and wrongs of their actions. Suffice it to say that these were early days in the charismatic movement and there was fear of disunity and distraction. Even David himself had questions.

By God's grace, his relationship with Mark remained intact and David continued to serve at the Round. In David's words once more: 'As I found myself unexpectedly homeless, Mark Ruston graciously took me in... Whatever private misgivings Mark may have had, I have always respected him for his patient and steady acceptance of me as a person, and our relationship over the years is something I have always treasured.'[7] Mark Ruston's friendship with David Watson during this difficult time says much about Mark's wisdom as a pastor. He was determined that the church should not be diverted from gospel-centred, word-centred, Christ-centred ministry and that it would not be divided on secondary issues. At the end of his curacy, David moved on from Cambridge having married Anne, a member of the church family. Mark continued to serve alongside, train and encourage the curates who followed David – several of whom have made contributions to this book.

Throughout his ministry, Mark was consistently committed to *prayer*, to *preaching* the whole counsel of God, and to caring for *people* in such a way as to present everyone 'mature in Christ'. What he asked God to do for others, he modelled in his own life, from the early days.

Gordon Bridger was a curate at the Round (1960–62), former principal of Oak Hill Theological College (1987–96) and served in churches in London, Edinburgh and Norwich. He is now retired and a member of the preaching team at Cromer Parish Church.

Canon Mark Ruston was a very good friend. I lived with my family in St John's Street, Cambridge, opposite the Round Church, while he was vicar there. I had not been baptised in my infancy, though I attended church occasionally. My husband, son and daughter had been baptised and I was beginning to feel an outsider.

In 1946 I had become a friend of the writer Dorothy L. Sayers, who was then translating Dante's 'Divine Comedy' for Penguin Classics. She often came to stay with me and we discussed Dante together. I began to read her own works, not only her detective novels but also her articles on Christianity. The two influences – the sermons and ceremonies at the Round Church, combined with the vigour and clarity of Sayers's writing – brought me to a point of decision. I telephoned Mark Ruston and asked him if he would be willing to baptise me.

He came to see me and was very helpful. He explained that I would need three witnesses, and I wrote to Dorothy Sayers to ask if she would be one. She replied that this would give her much pleasure, and said that she noted that the Prayer Book called them godparents. The ceremony took place at the Round Church on 13 December 1957. My father and aunt and Dorothy Sayers were my godparents. Mark Ruston presided. Afterwards a tea party was held in my flat, to which Mark Ruston came.

Dorothy Sayers was my guest at the Blue Boar Hotel and she left the following morning. On the 18 December I received a letter from her, expressing her pleasure at being my godmother. That very morning I had received a telephone call from her secretary telling me that she had died suddenly of a heart attack the previous day. My grief was profound and Mark Ruston was very sympathetic. Her publishers asked me to complete her translation of Dante (13 cantos of 'Paradiso'), a formidable task which took me two years. During that period I benefited greatly from the spiritual help of Mark Ruston. When I had completed the work I sent him a copy, and he wrote to me as follows: 'What a revolution God's grace can accomplish in six years! Philippians 1:6 is my verse for you. "Being confident of this very thing, that he which hath begun a good work in you will perform it until the day of Jesus Christ."' [8]

Barbara Reynolds, member of the Round in the 1950s and 1960s, former Lecturer in Italian at Cambridge University, Dante scholar, now a member of St Andrew's, Chesterton.

Endnotes

1. Mark was born on 23 August 1916; he was an undergraduate student at Jesus College, graduating with a BA in 1939; a theological student at Ridley Hall (1939–40). Subsequently, he served a curacy at St John's, Woking (1940–42); chaplain of Cheltenham College (1942–51); chaplain of Jesus College, Cambridge (1951–53); chaplain of Emmanuel College, Cambridge (1953–54); curate at St Paul's, Cambridge (1954–55); vicar of the Church of the Holy Sepulchre, Cambridge, known as 'The Round' (1955–87); he was also Rural Dean (1974–81), Honorary Canon of Ely Cathedral (from 1975), Chaplain to Her Majesty the Queen (from 1980); Mark retired in April 1987; and died on 3 January 1990. (taken from Crockford's, 1985–86).

2. Thanks to Stephen Walley (who, for many years, was responsible for producing the Round Church Magazine) for locating this photograph and for help with other aspects of research.

3. Islington Week is now called 'London Week' and is run by the Proclamation Trust. London Week is a programme for students who may be considering full-time gospel ministry. They are placed with a ministry family in London, living and serving with them in the busy run-up to Christmas; and spend the mornings at the Proclamation Trust's London base, learning about Christian service.

4. 'After three years at St Mark's, Gillingham, I went back to Cambridge for my second curacy, deliberately accepting an invitation to a totally different parish, the Round Church, for the purpose of widening my experience. I had no idea that the next three years would contain some of the most thrilling, confusing, traumatic and painful experiences of my life.' Watson, David. *You Are My God*, Hodder & Stoughton, 1983, p. 48.

5. Watson, ibid, p. 49.

6. Watson describes it in these terms: 'a quiet but overwhelming sense of being embraced by the love of God... no startling manifestations... I *knew* I had been filled with the Spirit... I was bubbling over with new joy.' Watson, ibid, p. 54.

7. Watson, ibid, pp. 65–66.

8. Quoted from the King James Version.

CHAPTER 3

Building up the church (1965 to 1987)

Robin & Marian Porter Goff

A few months before he retired, Mark Ruston wrote in the church magazine: 'In what order would we put "building up Christians" and "winning others for Christ"? I would put these two as twin aims.' And so he did, with faithful prayer and sacrificial caring.

Arriving at the Round Church in 1970, we found a unique church building, eccentric hall facilities, no vicarage, compromise solutions for the church office, but a warm welcome on our first Sunday morning. Over the coming years, we saw a number of groups develop to teach and encourage members of the church family and to promote Mark's aims. He longed to disciple believers who would bring others to Christ.

Building up Christians

The family service was becoming increasingly popular and eventually, as more space was needed, the smaller children were taken down to the local primary school in Park Street where there were better facilities for their classes. The fact that Mark Ruston was the chairman of the school governors and that two church members were also governors may have helped this arrangement. After the service, parents socialised over coffee in the school while the children took advantage of the playground.

In the 1970s, successive curates with responsibility for families in the church were appointed – David Huggett and Dennis Lennon, both family men. An energetic family service committee was also formed, its members proving tireless in building up the different aspects of families' and children's work. The 11–14 year-olds met as a *Pathfinder* group in the church hall. The older *Contact* group of fifth and sixth formers who hung out together on Friday evenings was well supported by students from Ridley Hall, a theological college in Cambridge where they were training for ministry. Parish assistants also helped during their short-term service on the church staff. The *Schoolmembers' Christian Association* (SCA) flourished under the leadership of Jonathan Fletcher and Roger Combes who inspired and challenged the fifth and sixth formers from different churches or none at all. One ex-member of SCA wrote to Mark Ruston in 1987: 'I often look back on my time at the Round with deep gratitude and am aware how much the present direction of my life depends on all the help I had throughout my teens.'

House groups – for Bible study and prayer – were established by the early 1970s. A note to Mark Ruston sums up the value of small group ministry: 'I have never ceased to be grateful that you steered me towards a house group very soon after I came to the Round for the first time. The group provided valuable support at a crucial point when I needed to get to know members of the congregation and to be reinforced in aspects of Christian living.' Daytime groups for women of all ages, with or without little children, were soon set up in various homes to which newcomers and overseas visitors were warmly welcomed. The Bible studies were occasionally led by junior staff or students training for ministry. This could be challenging. One such student had a disconcerting way of responding to a nervous contribution with, 'Yes, go on...' Another introduction to church family life was through *Hub*. Many in their twenties and thirties met regularly in a home, including fringe folk who were not ready for a home Bible study group. Many middle-aged people now remember those days as crucial to their Christian growth as they moved on to serve the Lord in new ways.

During the 1980s, *Link Lunches* were introduced for undergraduates. Regular church members welcomed the young men and women into their homes once a term. Students warmed to this initiative and were helped to think more about practical Christian living in the real world. An undergraduate who was later ordained wrote: 'The peculiar composition of the Round congregation makes this kind of fellowship necessary and besides, it's good fun.' For a few years, Friday buffet lunches were held in the hall. These appealed to those who lived or worked near the city centre. It was easy to meet new people there and possibly catch a word with a staff member.

To assemble the whole church together was always difficult. In 1983, a parish weekend away was arranged at Hengrave Hall, with Gordon Bridger as the first guest speaker, taking 'Prayer' as his subject. *Hengrave* became a biennial event through the rest of the 1980s, with parish family days in alternate years.

With every activity and initiative at the Round, planning had to change and adapt. Arrangements for families were improved. More and more people came to the second Sunday morning service and a relay was arranged for an overflow congregation in the upper church hall. In the short term, this expedient met the need for more space.

Parish mission and outreach

The academic year 1982 to 1983 was a prayerful time as a parish mission became a reality with Keith de Berry as speaker. It was also an important period for looking seriously at our attitudes to outreach. This was to become a major aspect of our church life to be worked out under Mark Ashton's visionary ministry. Soon prayer triplets developed as a foundation for the Billy Graham Mission in 1984.

There were also mission training classes in preparation for the events. New ideas opened up and we began to think more about people outside and how to win them for Jesus Christ. Each group was able to consider their strategy together and individuals became bolder as they spread the gospel among their friends.

Personal counsel and biblical preaching

As a lifelong bachelor, living in a Jesus College house at 37 Jesus Lane, Mark Ruston quietly used his own interests and resources to encourage and pastor a variety of folk. He had a small boat on the Ouse, he owned a box at the Albert Hall and he had access to Twickenham: sometimes he would take a student training for ministry with him or perhaps a couple of church members, sometimes a staff member would receive a gift of tickets to a concert or game. Each year, Mark undertook a two-week chaplaincy in Wengen during the skiing season for the Intercontinental Church Society. So from music to sailing by way of rugby and skiing, Mark's distinctive care for individuals had many features that reflected his own lifestyle.

In his home during university term, Mark had Sunday tea parties for undergraduates, two colleges at a time. One ex-student later wrote: 'I can still remember the verse on your mantelpiece, "Consider him lest ye become wearied..." It has been an encouragement on many occasions.' A succession of young men were his lodgers at number 37. They learnt about personal discipline and day-to-day godliness on the home front – and about using a butter knife.

Mark cared greatly about the older members of the congregation even though the main pastoring and provision for them he entrusted to others. Some were of advanced years and had made adjustments to share the vision of the fast-growing number of young families and students. One of Mark's simple ways of involving an older friend was to give them the name of a young person who really needed prayer. Harnessing their time and interest was renewing for everyone across the generations.

Mark Ruston's life-long ministry was devoted to bringing young people to a vital Christian faith and he saw the Round Church as strategically placed to achieve this aim. The pattern of his work seemed simple: biblical preaching and untiring personal counsel. He consistently encouraged men with a maturing faith to consider the call to Christian ministry; but he also took time to help those whose faith was shaken and to give practical support to those whose lives were falling apart.

Mark's preaching ministry was more influential than he may have appreciated at the time. One former student wrote:

> *I am writing to represent the many anonymous students*
> *for whom God's word was brought alive through the*
> *teaching given at the Round. Specifically the expository*
> *ministry, which you and your colleague undertook, gave*
> *me a grounding in Scripture and, perhaps more lasting*
> *still, an attitude to Scripture which has stood me in good*

stead to this day. You will know of students who decided
to enter the ministry and you may still be able to follow
their tracks; but how many others are there like me who
sat near the back in the Round (or in the hall across the
road)? Be assured that we too were listening and learning!

In the 1970s, Mark Ruston had a three and a half month sabbatical, travelling through Africa and going on to Papua New Guinea: every night except two he stayed with ex-Round Church folk. It was his humble joy to know that he had been used by the Lord to have a share in the spiritual development of so many people throughout the world.

A wise and strategic initiative

One of Mark's final initiatives, along with five other trustees, was to set up the Jesus Lane Trust[1] – a far-sighted plan to raise money 'to provide pastoral and counselling support for students' in Cambridge. The Trust had its first meeting in 1985 and the initial appeal was in early 1987. It was intended to establish a regular income and/or a large capital fund. It may be a commonplace idea today but it was wonderfully strategic for those days. Today's students continue to benefit from God's generosity and Mark's wise planning.

In April 1987, after nearly thirty-two years as vicar of the Round Church, Mark retired. His curate, Giles Walter, expressing his own confidence in the future of the Round Church, wrote, 'with a new man at the helm there will be, no doubt, new emphases alongside old strengths'. And so it was to prove. Mark Ashton succeeded Mark Ruston as vicar in the autumn of 1987 and about a year later, with the endorsement of the church council, he invited his predecessor to join the Round Church congregation. It says much for the humility and faith of both men that this happened – and, in the short period before his final illness, Mark Ruston was often at Sunday services.

Mark Ruston was widely respected. For his long and faithful ministry in Cambridge and for his vision of encouraging biblically-faithful pastors in the church, he has been spoken of as the Charles Simeon of his generation.

Robin and Marian Porter Goff have been members of the Round/
St Andrew the Great since 1970. Robin was a University Lecturer
in Engineering and a Fellow and Director of Studies at Fitzwilliam
College. Now, in retirement, he is a Life Fellow of Fitzwilliam; Marian
has run women's Bible studies for many years.

*In November 1971, I found myself sitting in Mark Ruston's small,
unprepossessing study in 37 Jesus Lane. Mark was telling me gently to trust
the promise of Revelation 3:20. It was news to me that Jesus had made any
promise in a book called Revelation and it was also news to me that I should
trust it. I had gone up to Cambridge in October that year an atheist who was
determined to be a rational human being. I had gone with a friend to hear
David Sheppard speak and, impressed, had joined a discussion group to look
at David Watson's 'My God is Real'. To my surprise, I found the evidence for
the character, the claims and the resurrection of Jesus of Nazareth persuasive.
If I was to continue to be a rational human being, then I should become a
Christian: that was the conclusion my reading of the evidence suggested and
so after many a discussion I prayed a prayer of commitment.*

*That first conversation in Mark Ruston's study addressed the issue of
Christian assurance, and I owe to Mark deep thanks for many wise pieces
of advice in my life. As my first vicar, Mark helped me see church as a
flawed group of people but also as a group that would help me to grow
and learn. I gave my first talk in the Round Church and I appreciated
Mark's calm, thoughtful, self-critical preaching and teaching. I enjoyed his
wry humour ('Where there's death, there's hope!') and his suspicion of the
over-confident: 'you can be more logical than biblical' he commented to one
colleague in danger of espousing a puzzling belief. Mark also encouraged
me to go forward for ordination and to go to Shrewsbury House Youth &
Community Centre in inner-city Liverpool to learn a bit more about real
life. When I mentioned to him that at the Shewsy I was getting to know
Jane Wood, the daughter of Maurice, his near lifelong partner in humour,
friendship and advice, Mark encouraged me in that relationship that later
led to marriage. I am very grateful to that wise vicar of 37 Jesus Lane, and
the promise of Revelation 3:20 has indeed proved true for me.*

Henry Corbett, undergraduate at the Round (1971–74), Vicar of
St Peter's Church and St John Chrysostom's Church, Everton; and
Warden of Shrewsbury House Youth & Community Centre.

Endnotes

1. The Jesus Lane Trust is a Registered Charity (No. 29201) and can be contacted via the StAG
website at www.stag.org/support-us/jesus-lane-trust ; by emailing jlt@stag.org; or by writing to The
Administrator, Jesus Lane Trust, St Andrew the Great Church, St Andrews St, Cambridge CB2 3AX.

CHAPTER 4

A time of change (1987 to 1993)

Giles Walter

Visitors to the Round in the late 1970s and early 1980s would
have found a church with reverent, traditional worship at the
main morning service, with well-applied biblical exposition at its
heart; large numbers of students, supported by a relatively small
but very faithful resident congregation; smaller gatherings at 9.30
a.m. and 6.30 p.m.; and the same gentle, wise, and godly pastor at
its helm. The focus on the student ministry was undiminished, but
it was undertaken on a greatly strengthened base – with a strong
families' work, and each age-group catered for in the on-going life of
the church. The years between Mark's retirement in 1987 and 1994,
when the congregation crossed the town centre and moved into
its new premises at St Andrew the Great, were years of enormous
change in the church's life.

New man

Mark Ruston had for quite some time been talking of the need
to find a younger successor, who would bring new ideas and new
energy for the future. Though the appointment was not for him to
make, no issue could have been closer to his heart, or occupied a
more prominent place in his praying as his retirement drew near.

His delight at the eventual outcome was shared by many others, both locally and further afield. Among those others I certainly numbered myself. All I knew, when joining the staff in 1986, was that we would not have gone far into 1987 before he retired, and the search for a new vicar at the Round would be underway. But it had been my quiet – and necessarily discreet – hope that Mark 1 (as we came to refer to him) would be replaced at the right time by Mark 2, a man of the same gospel convictions, but whose personality and style could hardly have been more different, and who had nurtured me with great faithfulness in my earliest Christian days.

The process that led to Mark Ashton's appointment was most unusual. For one thing, no external patron was involved: the Parochial Church Council (PCC) of the Round Church is its own patron, and therefore held sole responsibility, in consultation with the Bishop of Ely, for finding its next pastor. The PCC set up a working group which made enquiries and tried to identify possible suitable candidates. In the end some thirty-five letters were sent out to potential applicants, and the working group was asked to produce a shortlist from among those who expressed interest.

It was at that point that something happened which no-one who was involved has ever been quite able to explain. The working group met for an evening with the intention of forming a shortlist to bring to the PCC. That shortlist was never drawn up. Try as they might in the course of that evening, the members of the group found, with increasing frustration as the clock ticked on, that they were getting nowhere. It was not that they disagreed about rival lists: rather, no list seemed to make sense, and it looked as if they would have to give up and try again another day. But shortly before they disbanded, it was as if the mists cleared. All present found themselves saying that there was only one name that they felt able to commend to the PCC. Strangely, this conviction was not reached by careful consideration and comparison of alternatives. They just felt very deeply that this one name was the only name they should consider further.

The PCC, to its great credit, trusted the judgement of the working group and went along with its recommendation. Mark Ashton was approached and discussions followed. Before very long his appointment was announced, and in the late summer of 1987 he and Fiona moved into the new vicarage with their young family. The twenty-two years of his ministry at the Round therefore began with a very real sense of 'it seemed good to the Holy Spirit, and to us': we never doubted that this was God's doing, or that Mark Ashton was God's man for the Round.

New priorities

It was plain from the start that the new man meant business. He made it clear that he would be devoted to this new, local ministry. His work having kept him on the road for much of the previous six years, Mark Ashton now declined all external engagements for his first year, and buried himself instead in the church's life. At that early stage, to the surprise of some of us, he professed little interest in undergraduates. Prior to coming to Cambridge, he and Fiona had lived in Clapham, London, and had been instrumental in the growth of the youth group in their multi-racial local church. They had become deeply involved in the lives of these young people, many of whom lacked educational and other privileges. Cambridge students, by contrast, had often come from positions of comfort and personal advantage, and were not generally noted for their humility. Mark Ashton clearly missed the company of those youngsters, who not infrequently came up to Cambridge in the early years, sometimes in the form of a splendid steel band which certainly brought a new dimension to Christian gatherings.

At his retirement party, Mark Ruston had told those present that he really could not have had a better job, than that of being vicar of the Round Church for all those years. He then paused, and corrected himself: it was his curates who had really had the best job of all. 'So, if I could perhaps have been my own curate...' Many other areas inevitably occupied his time and energies, but his heart was never far from undergraduates. His successor had a different focus. Mark Ashton would preach forcefully to students, and would roast them over Sunday tea at the vicarage, often with stirring words from Romans 12 about living sacrificially for Christ. But for many years he would never see them one-to-one. One young man, a medic from Jesus College, took particular exception to this, set out to break the mould and was repeatedly turned away from the vicarage front door. His first action on graduation was to appear there once more, beaming with anticipation: a kind of updated version of the persistent widow. Mark Ashton roared with laughter, admitted defeat, and invited him in. He was never short of a sense of humour, and never made the mistake of taking himself too seriously. But he knew his priorities, and stuck to them.

New focus on Sunday mornings

It was the 9.30 a.m. family service that first felt the impact of the new broom. For many years it had been led by lay people, and it was unusual for the clergy to be there at all: they had celebrated Holy Communion at 8 o'clock and reappeared in plenty of time for the 11 o'clock. In the days when the church had two curates, the family service was entrusted to one of them and the student work to the other – but, since it was in capable hands, attendance at the family service had not been a priority for Mark Ruston. The new man brought a young family with him, which was surely a significant factor in the way things developed. But more importantly, Mark Ashton had a growing conviction, which before long came to be a kind of watchword for the church as a whole, that 'we become a better student church by becoming a better normal church'. His assertion, for instance, that nothing is more important in a Sunday gathering than the work in the crèche, certainly sounded a note that had not been heard before. He was as aware as anyone of the strategic importance of gospel ministry in the heart of the university; but he was also determined to focus on the heart of the local church, in order to support its focus on that particular mission field.

Not surprisingly, the 11 o'clock service was also quick to feel the impact of this new dynamic, and though numbers had held up quite well in the interregnum they began noticeably to grow again in Mark's early months. His commitment to pulpit ministry at that later service was such that on one memorable occasion even a cripplingly heavy cold, enough to keep others in bed for days, was no match for his determination: dosed with half the contents of the vicarage medicine cabinet, he forced himself up in time for that later service, and all present received from Luke chapter five a vivid picture of how Jesus began by asking Peter for his boat, but before long was asking for his life. At least one undergraduate followed suit that morning; there may well have been others. Sunday by Sunday, whatever the scriptural passage, we knew we were there to do business with God.

Growth in the 11 o'clock congregation brought its own problems. In the early 1970s, TV equipment had been brought into the Round, so that those who had not managed to squeeze into the church building could watch it relayed to the little hall on the other side of the road. At that time this was quite a technological coup, and it resulted in people being accommodated who would otherwise have had to be turned away. But by the mid-1980s it was no longer needed, not least because of the attractions of Roy Clements's remarkable Bible-teaching ministry at Eden Baptist Church. As numbers grew again at the Round, so voices began to be heard, calling for its re-introduction. Quite a number of people, students in particular, were being turned away from the church door for lack of space. Surely something should be done?

A 'problem' of growth

Looking back at Mark Ashton's years of ministry in Cambridge, this was perhaps the point at which his gift of leadership was most strikingly put to use. It is easy to look back over the way the church moved forward, into St Andrew the Great and beyond, as if there were all along a sense of inevitability about it. Nothing could have been further from the truth. A student training for ministry at Ridley Hall in the early 1990s made an off-the-cuff remark in Mark's hearing about how confident he was in his leadership role, and how he always knew where he was going. This comment, and others like it, irritated and annoyed him. There was no denying his strength of character or his leadership gifts. But he felt the weight of the great responsibility with which he had been entrusted: he never forgot his own sinfulness, fallibility and waywardness, and knew himself to be deeply dependent every step of the way on the Lord who had called him, if he were not to lead the church astray.

At this particular stage on the journey, Mark Ashton caused great consternation by refusing to allow the re-introduction of the relay to the church hall. PCC eyebrows – and voices – were not the only ones to be raised, as people were turned away from the main service, Sunday by Sunday. Something should indeed be done about it: but he was adamant that a TV relay was not that something. He had no more idea than anyone else, at the time, what the answer could be. But he insisted that setting up an overflow across the road would be a way of evading the real issue in front of us: namely, that the church was growing, and we needed to make proper provision for its on-going growth. To settle for a TV relay would be tantamount to a refusal to grow.

The strategic location of the Round was not to be lightly surrendered. But alternative large premises in the centre of Cambridge are not easy to come by. The substantial buildings of the Cambridge Union Society[1] were only a stone's throw away, on the same patch of land as the church, and were unoccupied on Sundays. But there was no question of their being available for Christian use. The Cambridge Inter-Collegiate Christian Union, which had for many years held its main meeting there each Saturday, had recently had to vacate it in order to make way for a weekly film night. The building had never been opened on Sundays since its construction in 1866. Further, we were given to understand that the caretaker prized his day off very highly, and would be so strongly opposed to any change of this kind that we would do better not to ask.

A move of God

Someone once observed that there is often a three-stage pattern to a real move of God: impossible; difficult; done. The move to the Union on Sunday mornings was of that kind. (The evening service continued in the old building, right up to the time of the move to St Andrew the Great.) People began to wonder whether a long-closed door might open, to accommodate this work of God. Mark Ashton expressed himself willing, if he had the church's support in prayer, to try gently leaning on it. Astonishingly, it began to give; and in the autumn of 1989, a mere six months from the time of the first enquiries, a combined 10.30 a.m. service in the debating chamber replaced the two morning services at the Round.

Mark Ashton disapproved strongly of rose-spectacled reminiscing. But it is hard not to indulge in a little at this point. Those early days in the Union were terrific. The families had never found the old building, with its massive pillars and minimal facilities, a congenial meeting-place, and they now revelled in the space and relative comfort of the Union. The students, who were perhaps less keen than their forebears to meet separately, clearly loved the fun and buzz of sharing a meeting with families and small children. The teaching was as central as ever: but child-friendly songs, sometimes with crazy actions, were as much a feature of the services as the sermon. The monthly all-together family service received no less attention than the others, because Mark Ashton believed passionately in the value of young and old sitting together under the ministry of the word. As he had inherited a congregation which was inflexible about the gospel, but flexible about most other things, remarkably few church members dropped out along the way. No-one who saw Sir Norman Anderson, then in his eighties, doing his best to bob up and down during a children's song is likely to forget it. Mark Ruston, who had by then rejoined the congregation at his successor's invitation, commented that it was all 'rather good, really', except that he was not sure he had seen any clergymen there. (Robes had been quietly laid aside sometime along the way.)

Mark Ashton's congregational research during his first year had shown him that, though church members loved much about the Round, and its teaching ministry in particular, they found many of the services to be dreadfully dull. Chanted psalms had been the order of the day for many years, and could still be heard in 1986. But by then they had come to symbolise the wide cultural gap between traditional worship and the expectations of modern students.

New focus on music

It so happened that Mark Ashton's arrival at the Round coincided with the arrival at Corpus Christi of a bright and irrepressibly dynamic young music student, whose contribution to the onward move of the church would turn out to be of great significance. Chris Hayward had spent his gap year learning about the place and practice of music in church life. In his early student weeks he cast his eyes around the local churches, decided that the Round was the one most in need of his attention, and moved in. Strange new things began to happen, somewhat to the consternation of more traditional folk. Never before had modern songs been accompanied at 11 o'clock by anything other than the organ, or the occasional guitar. Heads, some of them frowning, now peered around pillars, as the building reverberated to new sounds, with clarinets, oboes and others leading us in a thoroughly jazzed-up version of 'Thank you, Jesus'. The mould was well and truly broken.

Years later Chris and I would laugh about the almost impossible handful he had been in those early days. It is a measure both of the new vicar's discernment, and of his humility, that he recognised what God was giving to the church in the form of this new arrival. When Chris announced, towards the end of his second student year, that he had accepted the offer of a post at another Cambridge church from year three onwards, Mark Ashton simply said that he was depending on him, and could not undertake the move to the Union without him. There was no pleading, no pressure, and no flattery: just a simple statement of fact. It is a tribute to Chris, in his turn, that he chose wisely at that point, and stayed on board. His pastor had given him some hard times already, and there would be harder ones to come. Chris was surely aware of that, and knew he would have an easier ride elsewhere. But he also knew that Mark was utterly committed to him, to his welfare and to all that he could become, in Christ. So he stayed.

The move to St Andrew the Great, when it came, had never been Mark Ashton's idea. Building projects were close to being anathema to him, and he had thought he would leave the church if one were ever undertaken. In the event it was not so. That move, like everything else that was good over those seven years, was the Lord's doing. But he had his servant in place, to bring it about: one who was totally devoted to his Saviour, and to us: and we knew it.

Giles Walter was an undergraduate at the Round (1972–76), Curate at the Round (1986–93), and is now Vicar of St John's, Tunbridge Wells.

I grew up living in a Cathedral close, sang as a chorister as a boy and then came up to Cambridge to be a choral scholar at King's College. I thought I had the religion ticket sorted – it was all about showing due deference, especially on a Sunday, and everything would probably end up OK. But then I met some students who behaved differently and who had a real and deep interest in Christianity – not as an intellectual subject, rather as a lifestyle choice. It was definitely the people rather than the church that made the difference for me. These people had deeply attractive personalities and I wanted to know more about what made them tick. They invited me to their church, the Round Church, which was meeting in the Union Society Debating Chamber because there were too many people to fit into the Round Church. (That in itself made it worth a visit.) I felt deeply uncomfortable throughout my first visits and yet what I heard I knew to be true – I heard for the first time the simple truths of the Christian message laid out clearly and straightforwardly. I began to understand that being a Christian was not about trying to be a good person, but accepting that I could never be 'good enough' and therefore needed serious help!

Despite the major cultural challenges with my preconceptions of what Christianity was all about I knew that I had to make a choice, and so I took the step and spoke to the curate, Giles Walter. Twenty-two years on, I remain totally convinced that this initial small step was the starting point of the greatest decision of my life – to follow Jesus.

Joss Sanders, undergraduate at the Round (1990–91), teacher, Brickhill Baptist Church, Bedford.

Endnotes

1. The Cambridge Union Society is a debating and social society for students from Cambridge University and Anglia Ruskin University. The Society's headquarters building behind the Round Church is known as The Union and houses the famous Debating Chamber.

CHAPTER 5

Moving to St Andrew the Great (1993 to 1994)

Peter Robinson

The Round Church is a unique and extraordinary building, held in great affection by those who know it well. But it was never designed with the size and needs of a modern congregation in mind. The large numbers of students who came to the Round Church during the university terms filled the building to capacity. A relay was installed to the hall on the other side of Round Church Street in the early 1960s, and this was extended to include closed-circuit television a few years later. This might seem obvious today, but it was unusual and advanced technology back in the 1960s and 1970s. We were fortunate to have Humphrey Hinton, an engineer with the Pye company, in the congregation to look after the system.

But huge stone pillars and TV relays between preacher and congregation are not helpful for effective Bible teaching. So, as the student ministry continued to prosper after the arrival of Mark Ashton in 1987, and was complemented by growth in the number of families with children at the earlier Sunday morning service, another solution was needed. So, as mentioned in Chapter 4, the Sunday morning services moved into the debating chamber of the Cambridge Union Society, just behind the church building. This proved remarkably successful,

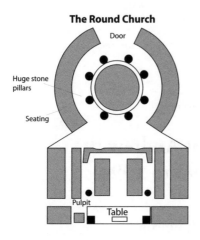

The Round Church

Door

Huge stone pillars

Seating

Pulpit

Table

This illustration shows the layout of the Round Church with the huge stone pillars between preacher and congregation – a building never designed for the size and needs of a modern congregation.

not least thanks to the talent of Chris Hayward, our director of music.

Numerous lessons were learned in the Union Society – many of which were significant in planning for the next phase of the church's life. We started in the Union with a single service, bringing the whole church together. However, the extra space we had gained was soon filled as the church grew; a full church is actually discouraging for newcomers, there should be empty seats near the door for tentative latecomers. So we divided into two services during term, but found that many students rather enjoyed coming to the earlier family service. We also started by rearranging the chairs so that they all faced the lectern, which was at one side of the room. However, we soon discovered that leaving the seating in 'parliamentary' arrangement so that two halves of the congregation faced each other was rather better. Christians meet on Sundays to encourage each other and it is much easier to do this when you can see their faces!

Challenges

However, there were still difficulties. There were the physical complications of setting up services every week and tidying afterwards. There were no storage facilities at the Union. All the sound and music equipment had to be carried from the Round Church to the Union building, set up and then carried back again – every Sunday, rain or shine. Service times and locations changed at the beginning and end of each term, which was particularly difficult for newcomers and occasional visitors. Children going to their Sunday morning activities still had to cross two busy roads to reach their classes in the local primary school.

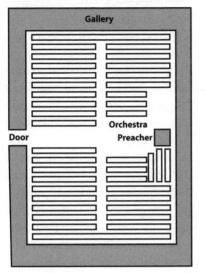

Cambridge Union Society Debating Chamber

Gallery

Orchestra

Door

Preacher

The layout of the Cambridge Union Society Debating Chamber, with its 'parliamentary-style' seating and gallery, where members of the congregation were able to see each other's faces, rather than backs of heads.

Meanwhile, a rather different problem was facing the Diocese, just along the road. The church of St Andrew the Great in central Cambridge had been closed some years earlier. Plans to reinstate it as a boutique shopping centre or as a tourist information centre failed to achieve planning permission or funding, and the building was deteriorating to the point that it was becoming dangerous to passers-by.

In October 1990, John Rose, one of the churchwardens, was having a conversation with the Archdeacon after a Diocesan meeting, when they both wondered about the possibility of the Round Church moving to St Andrew the Great. At the same time, Andrew Murdoch, a partner with the Fitzroy Robinson partnership of architects who had worked on the commercial development plans, approached his old friend Mark Ashton with the same suggestion. By the summer of 1991, a feasibility study had shown that the building could be restored and extended to accommodate over 700 people (with ten extra rooms for children's activities, kitchens, toilets and so on) for approximately £1,800,000. The whole church then had to face the question of how to proceed.

A spiritual project

The most important lesson that we learned is that building for a church is a spiritual project, and you should not expect to run it as you might run a conventional business project. For example, our most important decision was whether or not the project would serve the gospel in Cambridge rather than how it would be funded, and certainly not how it might improve our church meetings. It is perhaps significant that although I am (fairly) numerate, I have no formal financial qualification, and yet was invited to oversee the financial aspects of the project.

I personally found it very helpful that we had drafted a vision statement for the church a year or two earlier. This identified our commitment to the Bible and to prayer, our special mission to students in Cambridge, and our commitment to individual and corporate growth. The original phrasing was a bit more verbose, but the intention was the same. I was convinced that the project would allow us to minister better to students while building up the 'resident' congregation to make church plants possible subsequently. It also convinced me that this was a proper use of so much of the church's money and, indeed, helped my wife Carol and me work through the personal matter of contributing our share of the cost.

A wise member of the church council said that we should only undertake the project if we could be certain that not one soul would be lost through the distraction caused by building. We can never know if this was achieved, but one consequence was that Mark Ashton had no involvement with the day-to-day design and financial planning for the building; he was kept free to continue teaching the Bible. The project was led by John Rose with assistance from Auriel Schluter, Catherine Twentyman (now Meijer, who was employed half-time on the project) and me. We were joined by Roger Gooden, another Christian architect from Fitzroy Robinson and the only professional on the management team.

Prayer and finances

The real point about our decision to proceed was that it was only partly guided by financial criteria, and mostly by a strong sense of God's will. It took us one year to identify what might be possible and another year to convince ourselves that it was God's will. This included taking the church away on a retreat for a weekend, weekly prayer meetings and a couple of half nights of prayer. Weekly prayer meetings continued to play a crucial role throughout the project. After that, we couldn't really *not* proceed. We are still paying the bills almost twenty years later, but it is absolutely clear that the decision was right. The pain of raising the money was nothing compared to the pain of three subsequent church plants, but it has been wonderful to watch the gospel prosper in Cambridge.

We had a legacy of £25,000 just as the possibility first arose in 1990, and we used this to underwrite the costs of the initial feasibility studies. The church council decided in principle to pursue the project in November 1991, and made personal commitments totalling £250,000 by the end of the year. We then asked the whole church membership to make commitments in February 1992.

The church council met on 17 February 1992, the day after the Gift Day. Catherine Twentyman and I had spent the whole day keying people's responses into a computer so that we could add up the amount offered and calculate the effects of tax recovery. Finally, at about 7.00 p.m., we pushed the button and saw a total of £700,000 plus £200,000 in tax refunds. We sat there awestruck for a few moments and then broke into prayer. No-one else on the church council (not even John Rose) knew this when they decided on how much should have been raised before we started.

When the church council met, we did not have exact figures for either the cost of the project or the money that would be released by selling property. However, John and I wanted to establish the principles by which we could place contracts without having to return to the church council. We envisaged dividing the building contract into three parts – essential works, work that could be deferred, and optional extras. The church council decided that we could only sign a contract if we were sure that the essential works were fully covered by the income from property, the external appeal, and the congregation. I then announced the outcome of the initial Gift Day and it was clear that we would proceed with both the essential and deferred works.

Rather more than half of the gifts were in cash and the remainder in four-year covenants. The core membership of the church – those belonging to home groups – consisted of about 130 people, so this involved some quite significant sacrifices. In particular, people gave from their capital reserves rather than from their current income. Many families went without holidays for a year or two, and young couples postponed starting their families. We had also arranged to sell our old church hall privately and to sell our curate's house to the Diocese, together raising a further £250,000. We anticipated raising a further £100,000 from the congregation, £100,000 from a public appeal and

£400,000 from commercial use of the Round Church building. At that point we started building.

In the event, the public appeal only realised about £30,000, most of which was a grant from the City Council. We did receive a grant from a charitable trust, but that was to support an additional minister in the new building, which did not help the finances but confirmed the importance of ministry through people rather

Mark Ashton speaking to the church family on the morning of Sunday, 6 September 1992, when members of the congregation walked in the rain from the Round Church to St Andrew the Great and prayed for God's blessing on their proposed move from one building to the other.[2] (Reproduced with the permission of the Cambridge News)

than through buildings. So we had to ask the church members for more money after we had started building, and they cheerfully gave again in November 1993, bringing their contribution up to £1.3 million. It seemed entirely natural to invite John Chapman to lead a one-week mission in the new building during January 1994, a couple of months before we moved in completely. A giant banner proclaiming 'People restore buildings, God restores lives' along the scaffolding round the building attracted plenty of attention.[1]

After another two or three years, English Heritage blocked commercial use of the Round Church building, despite our having approval from both the Diocese and the City Council. The finances survived thanks to a loan of £500,000 from the Diocese to be repaid (with interest) over twenty years, but we still had to turn to the congregation yet again to bring the debt under control.

We still have about £20,000 of the Diocesan loan outstanding, but we hope to clear this before it becomes due in 2014. Meanwhile the church's finances continue to be a witness to God's grace, and the congregation's generosity a witness to their faith. It was and is humbling to watch the way God works though a project like this. I rather enjoyed being asked on local television how we had raised £1.8 million and being able to reply in all honesty that we had the advantage of being a church that believed in miracles. It would be easy to claim that the Round Church had a wealthy congregation, but in truth there were very few city executives and entrepreneurs, just a lot of faithful Christians who were happy to return what God had given them.

As part of the feasibility study early in 1991 we invited Michael Baughen to come and speak to us about his experiences overseeing a massive building project as rector of All Souls, Langham Place, in London during the 1970s. He started by saying that he was thrilled about what we were proposing, not because of what would be built physically, but because of how it would build us as God's people. I did not really understand what he meant at the time, but I do now. Of course, he was absolutely right. A building project is only worth doing if it builds the congregation spiritually as well.

Addendum: A lady called Margaret Welch was a member of the original church at St Andrew the Great. When services there were suspended in the 1970s, she and a group of half a dozen or so people met regularly to pray that the building might come back to life as a church. Although our churchmanship was very different, she was thrilled when we revived the building in the 1990s. She died in 2010 and left a considerable bequest to St Andrew the Great, allowing the Diocesan loan to be paid off. This also allowed Mark Ashton to achieve one of his ambitions, albeit posthumously, by passing on a church in a sound financial state to his successor.

Peter Robinson has been a member of the Round/St Andrew the Great since 1980; he is Professor of Computer Technology at Cambridge University.

I feel that it was an immense privilege to have been involved in the move from the Round to St Andrew the Great, because it was a time when we witnessed God working miracle upon miracle. It seems to me that it began with a miracle when God put the 'idea' of the move into the heads of two such different people, one a member of the church, and the other the architect who had originally been taken on to turn the building into a shopping area. And the miracles continued as obstacles were removed one by one. Two things stand out in my mind, one is the way in which God answered prayer, and the second the joy we experienced in giving.

It was lovely at the outset to discover that we were the answer to the prayers of a few faithful people who had once attended St Andrew the Great and who had been praying for many years that it would one day be used again for the glory of God. Those few came regularly to our prayer meetings while remaining faithful to the churches they had joined when St Andrew the Great had been closed. They were a constant source of encouragement. Then, as the project got under way, we saw our prayers being answered time after time. We would pray on the eve of some special decision and then be almost surprised that our prayers were answered. I remember, for instance, when we prayed that the Diocese would allow us to have a baptistry. At the time we had a rather unfortunate, huge font, and we were amazed and thankful when the Diocese said that we could have a baptistry, but not both a baptistry and a font (the font was put to good use; another fellowship was on the lookout for one). A small example, but God answered our prayers, both great and small, as the building was rescued from the 'hard-hat site' we first visited into the building it is today.

Then the joy we experienced in giving. We were blessed with marvellous teaching about giving by both of the Marks – not for them 'fund-raising' but consistent teaching about responsible giving by God's people and the reminder that we are only giving back what he gave us in the first place. We were not a wealthy congregation at that time and people must have given sacrificially, as Peter has said, but I never saw long faces. There was one memorable Gift Day when we were right into the project and large sewage pipes loaned by the builders were set up for us to put our gifts into. (On another occasion, we used a cement mixer.) Everyone loved it, not least the children, and people's faces shone as they went forward with their gifts.

Cecily Rose, member of the Round/St Andrew the Great since 1980 and on the staff as women's worker/church secretary (1980–96) (and widow of John Rose, who was the member of staff with special responsibility for the move to St Andrew the Great).

Moving to St Andrew the Great – 1993 to 1994

Endnotes

1. Some key dates in the move to St Andrew the Great: the possibility of moving into the St Andrew the Great building was originally considered in October 1990 with a first discussion meeting held on 5 November 1990. An open day for the congregation was held at St Andrew the Great on Sunday, 10 March 1991. A church retreat at Hengrave Hall took place from Friday, 14 June to Sunday, 16 June 1991 to talk and pray about the possibility of a move. In the summer of 1991, a feasibility study was conducted. The team consisting of John Rose, Auriel Schluter, Catherine Twentyman (now Meijer), Peter Robinson and Roger Gooden (the architect) met regularly during that autumn. The first Gift Day was held on Sunday, 16 February 1992 and the church council took the decision in principle to proceed on Monday, 17 February 1992. Tenders were invited over the summer of 1992. On Sunday, 6 September 1992, the congregation walked from the Round Church to St Andrew the Great and prayed for God's blessing on the proposed move. Work started on the building on Monday, 7 September 1993. Building work continued through 1993 and another Gift Day was held on Sunday, 7 November 1993. The building work was originally intended to be completed by the end of 1993 and a week-long mission with John Chapman was planned for Tuesday, 18 January to Sunday, 23 January 1994. In the event, the building work was not completed by then but the builders vacated the building for the week and the mission went ahead. The first Sunday service in the newly restored building was on Sunday, 6 March 1994.

2. Among those visible in the photograph are Frank Price, Chris, Clare and Nick Ashton, Mary Juckes (now Davis), Richard James, Veronica Glauert, Norman Anderson, Elizabeth Rayment, Philip McNair, Joan Bowen, Tim Holland, Judy Coe, Suzanne Laurence and Hugh Dircks, Rhonda Wilson, Lesley McFall, Paula and Mark Ayliffe, Stephen Oakley, Humphrey Hinton, Leslie-Ann Parker, Helen and Chris Wingfield, Mary Vertue, Mark, Anna and Peter Robinson, Mark Ashton.

PART 3

THE STORY OF ST ANDREW THE GREAT (1994 TO 2010)

Here the story is told by focusing on six different areas of ministry. Again, it is a snapshot and looks at areas of ministry that have arisen because of where St Andrew the Great (StAG) is placed – right in the heart of the city of Cambridge. There are, of course, many areas of ministry which are not covered here (work with families, youth and children, with 20s & 30s, and the retired; Bible study groups; music ministry; and so on). Rather than being exhaustive, this chapter tries to highlight just some of the ministry opportunities and the ways in which God has been graciously working in this particular local church.

Chapter 6

Serving the students – three perspectives

Roger Combes, Giles Walter & Brian Elfick

This chapter on student work starts by looking back. Student work was a priority for this church fellowship from Mark Ruston's earliest days at the Round – and Roger Combes speaks for this generation and puts today's student work in its context. The aims of those involved in seeking to serve the students in Cambridge over five decades have remained constant and are well summed up by Colossians 1:28, 'We proclaim him (Jesus), admonishing and teaching everyone with all wisdom, so that we may present everyone perfect in Christ.' The way the church has sought under God to fulfil that aim has varied over the years. Three curates – Roger Combes, Giles Walter and Brian Elfick – share their perspectives.

Student work in 1970s and 1980s

Mark Ruston once said to me that he somehow knew that he 'would always be working with children or students'. It is a wonderful thing both to know where one's gifts lie and to have an opportunity to exercise them under God's blessing. It was certainly true of Mark. I remember inviting him to give a talk on the Pathfinder Venture that I was leading with students and members of the Round at

Wimborne one summer. He arrived to give his talk equipped with a power sander and extension lead, and it was inspiring to see this man well into his sixties with these young boys on the edge of their seats and fully participating. On other occasions he came out to the annual house party for thirty Cambridge fifth and sixth formers to give another excellent practical talk to the absorbed young audience.

Mark Ruston was a shy man and his ministry with students self-effacing, yet he had the ability to win the confidence of supremely confident and able people. Keith Sutton, later to be Bishop of Lichfield, said he had a special gift of being able to bring people into the kingdom. Beyond that, Mark was also a wise and trusted counsellor to young people on their path to Christian maturity and through different kinds of personal difficulties.

The Cambridge Inter-Collegiate Christian Union

He was also a trusted figure on the wider Christian student scene in Cambridge. Although he was rarely asked to give the 'Bible Readings' for the Cambridge Inter-Collegiate Christian Union (CICCU), he was an elder statesman with whom the CICCU executive members could consult. This did not happen invariably and there were periods when no doubt Mark Ruston wished it happened more. But after the three-yearly missions which the CICCU organised, Mark would usually be the person who was asked, perhaps with others, to speak at a four or six-session course for those who had recently embraced the Christian faith. These talks would be informal, clear, practical and disarmingly un-intense.

I was fortunate to come to Ridley Hall in 1971 and to be part of CICCU for the next three years including involvement in the 1974 David MacInnes mission. In these years the CICCU was strong in the attendance that it could command on Saturday evening 'Bible Readings' (400 attending would not be unusual) and an evangelistic address intended for Christian students to bring their friends to on Sunday evenings, often 200–300 people. At one time I reckoned there were 1,000 undergraduates in the university involved in the college weekly Bible study groups under the auspices of CICCU. Hundreds of students were also engaged in what were called evangelistic groups, which in those days would be discussing typically a chapter of David Watson's book *My God is Real*[1], which proved a very effective evangelistic tool.

With this quick sketch of the CICCU in the 1970s and 1980s and of Mark Ruston himself, we can see how the Round tried to serve students of that time.

Aims and strategies

This was before the days of vision and mission statements, at the Round at any rate. I have no memory of sitting down to hammer out a strategy for work among students. The aim, I just assumed, was to bring students to Christ and to present them mature in Christ. Perhaps the nearest I heard to a strategy was Mark Ruston saying that he aimed not to do anything in church life that would draw students away from CICCU involvement.

Mark Ruston expected the student curate to work mainly among undergraduates (and older teenagers). He was free to make contact with those students who attended the Round and, when invited, to speak to college Christian Union groups. In time, Mark added a noble succession of parish assistants, particularly for female students.

The 'town' congregation at the Round might have been surprised how much they were providing a welcoming church family for undergraduates on Sunday mornings. In nearly eleven years at the Round, at Ridley and as curate, I cannot remember a single member of the church making a resentful comment about students in the church. In fact, the congregation realised that they were providing a base that would benefit these students in their Christian life, and they were pleased to do so and back it up with prayer, finance and friendliness. Some people baked scones and cakes for student teas several times a term, year after year, without ever seeing them being appreciated. Student Lunch Sundays, introduced in the early 1980s, were popular with students and the homes which hosted them. Otherwise, the main contact students had with the Round would be the Sunday morning service. In term-time every week, some would be fortunate enough to have the encouragement of a coffee or tea with Mark Ruston. Someone once said of his preaching, that you think he is giving you a gentle talk, and afterwards you find you've been hit for six!

The 70s Group, later named *The Simeons,* was a group Mark convened once a term for students considering the ordained ministry. Mark had the names of some 200 students from this group over the years who had gone on to be ordained (though a few of these would have come from other churches or college chapels).

The standard of the CICCU preachers and teachers on Saturday and Sunday evenings (and often at the Round on Sunday morning) was very high at this time. One Union Society president of the time – Peter Harvey – recommended members to go to CICCU meetings to learn about public speaking. The talks were varied, accessible, applied, positive and always faithful to the biblical revelation. It was only a small step from believing in the power of the word preached to decide that the most strategic ministry I could exercise among students was to get them to where they would be blessed. The Saturday 'Bible Readings' brought sane and challenging teaching to young lives, and the Sunday evening address was an effective way for many to start to bring others to hear the gospel. Those students who exposed themselves like this to the challenge of the Bible expounded and applied at weekends gained hugely for their future faith and service. It undergirded their college Christian Union groups and Sunday church (and college chapel for some, hopefully) and laid deep foundations in many lives. The student's capacity for intellectual development is of course immense in undergraduate years. But one felt one could see them growing spiritually too – almost week by week!

So helping students to receive what CICCU and their college groups had to offer became a main thrust of the Round's ministry. Several of us curates and parish assistants can remember going days without having lunch, coffee or tea on our own. Sometimes these one-to-one chats with students would be doing more the work of an evangelist, sometimes more as an encourager, trying to strengthen them in their Christian life or in their helping of others.

The purpose of a Christian Union

One particular thing I found often helped a student was to understand what a Christian Union was for. How did a Christian Union fit in with everything else in university life? What was the brief of a Christian Union? It was easy to be bemused by it all.

To get some clarity on these unspoken questions could liberate a person into joyful and effective fellowship that would be a lasting blessing for them and others. An understanding that a Christian Union has only a limited aim could be encouraging, and help people to commit to it and enjoy its benefits. My understanding was something as follows, and I frequently passed it on, for what it was worth:

For only a short time (three years, and in eight-week bursts) a Christian Union unites Christian students who choose to unite around four tenets of their faith, viz:

- Christianity is Christ
- The Bible is God's word to human beings
- The cross is the way to God
- Individuals need to respond to God's gospel

Not all Christian students wish to unite around these points, and Christian Union members will quite properly differ greatly on styles of worship, church organisation or in other ways. But if they can accept and respect these differences among themselves, and unite around the four tenets above, it can greatly strengthen their witness to Christ among their contemporaries for the short, artificial time they are together. This was the sort of understanding that lay behind the Round's work among students. Cambridge Inter-Collegiate Christian Union has been the early training ground of Christian men and women, including countless leaders, for well over 100 years. 'Pumping out committed men and women into the world' as one Divinity School lecturer said.

The privilege for the Round was to be able to support this, 'a pillar and foundation of the truth', as 1 Timothy 3:15 describes the church. It was a great privilege for me to be part of the Round in all this, and to see individuals and college groups discovering the grace of God and passing it on to the next (student) generation.

Roger Combes was Curate at the Round (1977–86) and is now Rector of St Matthew's, St Leonards-on-Sea and Archdeacon of Horsham, Chichester diocese.

My spiritual birth was at Cambridge where so many different people pointed me towards Jesus. In spite of two and a half terms of resistance, God continued to call and draw me, and my crunch week of decision and new birth involved my first trip to the Round Church where I underlined a commitment I had made a couple of days earlier. Strangely, in my 'resistance' I had heard a voice inside saying, 'George, you must become a Christian!' But I think it was my understanding of the rationale of it all (I was studying Maths!), and particularly the atonement with Jesus taking my place on the cross. When I went to the Round Church, Mark Ruston was leading and Keith de Berry was preaching. I put my name on a piece of paper afterwards, declaring that I had made my decision for Christ.

Roger Combes, the curate, encouraged me and, from that first day, I was walking with Jesus, setting aside time to pray and to read the Bible. The Round became my church in term-time from that week on and helped to give me a solid biblical foundation to go on in discipleship and mission, and Roger even persuaded me to go and help on a Scripture Union Christian venture (Iwerne Minster) that summer. I thank God for the Round, for Mark Ruston, Roger and Keith speaking that day, as it was through them as well as Cambridge Inter-College Christian Union that I was pointed in The Way.

George Newton, undergraduate at the Round (1982-84), now Vicar of Holy Trinity Church, Aldershot.

Student work in the 1980s and 1990s

Anyone who has been involved in ministry among university students will echo Roger Combes' verdict, that such involvement is a huge privilege. It has long been so for the Round Church corporately, and for individuals who have the happy task of giving the bulk of their own time and energy to such ministry. Coming to the Round as I did in 1986 from a suburban London parish, to be told by Mark Ruston that he expected me to spend ninety per cent of my time on student ministry was music to my ears. When I cautiously asked him whether I might accept an invitation from a college Christian group to join them for a few days away before the Michaelmas term, he eagerly encouraged me to go on two such 'pre-terminals', if I could. I got the message.

A time to grow

Life in the undergraduate world moves at a fast pace and, in the life of a Christian student, those three years from arrival to graduation can be, and often are, hugely significant. I remember a speaker telling a group of students that God intended them to grow *fast* in their university years. Experience would seem to bear out the truth of his comment. The parable of the sower warns us against superficial enthusiasm. But there is every opportunity, in those highly formative years, for a young believer to put roots down deeply into the word of God and thereby lay the foundation for a lifetime of discipleship. For one who comes to faith early in their Cambridge years, there could hardly be a more privileged context in which to learn and grow.

Aims

From 1986, when Roger left the Round, to 1994, when the congregation moved into its new building at St Andrew the Great (StAG), our way of working with students continued much as previously: supporting and helping key players in the Cambridge Inter-Collegiate Christian Union; offering training sessions in evangelism and in Bible study leadership; encouraging students to make the most of what the Christian Union had to offer; feeding as many as possible into some form of Christian service in the summer vacation; and holding out before them the possibility of full-time ministry of some kind in the longer term.

The approach of the team at Eden Baptist church was very similar. The student congregation at Eden at the time was certainly as large as that at the Round, maybe larger; but Roy Clements, as a former staff worker for UCCF (Universities & Colleges Christian Fellowship), and Mark Dever, his formidably competent side-kick, while delighted to see them on Sunday mornings, stopped short of laying on anything further by way of a church-based student programme. A happy and good-natured rivalry existed between the two churches: we looked after different students, but had the same basic approach to their nurture and development.

The beginnings of a student team

And yet there were changes. In September 1986 the staff at the Round consisted of vicar, curate, honorary parish worker and two parish assistants. The role of the latter was definitely a subservient one. It involved some opportunity of ministry among students, but was essentially a practical role, involving a multitude of little tasks, the buying of Mr Ruston's favourite cheese being one of them. Anne Harris had given up a well-paid job teaching English in a private school and exchanged it for the role of parish assistant with little more than pocket money for remuneration. That she should have been willing to do this was a great testimony to her godly servant-heartedness.

In the course of Anne's second year with us there was a strong feeling among many people that she should be kept on the staff as a properly salaried, full-time worker with female undergraduates. So the new role of Women's Associate Student Pastor was proposed. An explanatory leaflet was produced, funds flowed in and Anne remained on the staff in that new capacity. Her life would be tragically cut short in a car accident several years later. But she exercised a wonderful ministry at the Round before returning to teaching after three years.

The team would grow a little more over the next few years. We were still a long way from the army of workers operating from StAG today. But the journey of a thousand miles begins with a single step, and Anne's appointment was a significant development.

Students training for ministry at Ridley Hall were also a great asset in the work. There was nothing new in this, as such; a Ridley man had always been attached to the Round by way of pastoral placement. But now the scale became different. Instead of the one, or possibly two, that had been allocated before, Mark Ashton badgered and cajoled the folk at Ridley into letting him have as many as half a dozen. They were each given different areas of ministry, but invariably had a concern for spiritual welfare of students, and would meet up with them for one-to-one Bible study, just as Mark Ashton had done with me in 1973, when he himself was training for ministry at Ridley. Further, we began to involve church members, mostly in their twenties, in similar partnerships. Much quiet, unobtrusive discipleship took place in this way.

Support for students

Little by little we began to offer more by way of structured support for the Cambridge Inter-Collegiate Christian Union (CICCU). Mark Ruston, now retired, was no longer in place to offer his wonderful, avuncular talks on the basics of Christian faith and life. So *Essentials*, an equivalent but slightly longer version of the same thing, became a regular feature of life at the Round. Then, at the end of the Lent term in 1991, we laid on a weekend away for first year students, using a hospitable Christian guest-house in the Fens for the purpose. The announcement of 'lights out at 10.00 p.m.' on the first night was greeted initially by disbelief, then by appreciation. The usefulness of the next day was greatly enhanced by that simple adjustment to the timetable.

The annual 'first years' weekend became a fixture thereafter. They were small gatherings, not many more than twelve to fifteen students, plus members of the team. But they were peculiarly happy and constructive ones, and played their part in directing some undergraduates towards full-time ministry in later life. Reading weeks in a north Norfolk windmill (the mill was no longer active!) also made their way into the programme, in the aftermath of graduation each year.

Student teas on Sunday afternoon at 37 Jesus Lane, Mark Ruston's home, continued until his retirement. It had long been a tradition for Christian students from a specified college to be invited on any given Sunday, to enjoy the hospitality of the vicarage and devour the scones and cakes so uncomplainingly provided by older members of the congregation. Sunday teas continued for a while at the new vicarage, with the added ingredient of a brief talk on the Bible, well aimed at student level, given either by Mark Ashton or by another member of the team. One consequence of Mark Ashton's high view of the centrality of the Bible in God's purposes was that he doubted the usefulness of any such occasion, if the Bible was not opened at some point. Newcomers' evenings for adults arriving at the church had likewise to include a brief talk from Scripture, and the same went for the senior members' tea.

Senior members of the church instinctively met for tea, but the habit was becoming something of a rarity in the life of an undergraduate. Lunch, however, was a different matter entirely.

So teas eventually gave way to Sunday lunches in the distinctly cramped quarters of the little hall across the road from the Round. Limitations of space meant that colleges continued to be invited by rota. A talk was always included, but only a brief one, and there was no consistent teaching programme for speakers to follow. Clearly things could have been done more effectively, and would be in due course. But, again, the seed of something new had been sown.

New dimensions?

In those years, kind observers of the student ministry at the Round began to be heard questioning the adequacy of this inherited model of student ministry for the new generation. Non-Christians, as likely as not, had never read something as basic as Mark's gospel, and, if they came to evangelistic meetings, would look quizzically at that little book on their seat. Professing Christian students would often arrive at the university with very limited Bible knowledge. If they were to leave the university in a similar state, we would not have done our job properly. On one occasion an older, very discerning church member challenged me directly, as to how solid a doctrinal foundation our way of doing things was giving to Christian students. The first part-time curate to join us from Australia openly doubted the adequacy of the modern-day CICCU to that task. Over in Oxford, St Aldate's under Michael Green had become far more proactive in its approach to student ministry. Perhaps it would soon be time, with new premises on offer at StAG, to add new dimensions to the work.

Giles Walter was an undergraduate at the Round (1972–76), Curate at the Round (1986–93), and is now Vicar of St John's, Tunbridge Wells.

I was a final year student and had been having lengthy discussions about Christianity with a fellow student, Ed. Christ had no place in my life and my view of religion was extremely negative. Despite this, Ed persuaded me to come along to his church, the Round. I was surprised by this large vibrant church full of young people in the middle of town. The sermons seemed to be written specifically for me and were really speaking to me.

After a couple of weeks Ed encouraged me to go along to the four week 'Essentials Course'. Two staff members, Mary Juckes (now Davis) and Ian Garrett, were running this particular course that gave those of us attending an opportunity to discuss the basics of Christianity. Within a couple of weeks God was really opening my eyes to the gospel and it was at the Cambridge Inter-Collegiate Christian Union mini-mission, where Mark Ashton was speaking, that I became convinced that I was a sinner and that the only way to God was through Jesus Christ. After being enthralled by what Mark was speaking about, I realised that I had a choice to make. I went to speak to Mark after the service. I proudly told him I had been coming along to his church and going to the Essentials Course. He looked at me and all he said was 'Karen, don't leave it in the in-tray too long.' I was surprised by his response at the time but in hindsight see that it was an extremely wise statement designed for my salvation. I needed to take a decision and that night I chose to give my life to Christ.

Mary continued to meet with me for weekly Bible studies for the next two years while I finished my course and was President of the Student Union at Anglia Polytechnic University (now Anglia Ruskin University). What a privilege to be given such input, teaching and support that has grounded me in Christ and equipped me to serve. To me, this showed the Round Church's commitment to make disciples of all nations and equip students in leadership and godly service.

Karen Halls (née Decker), member of StAG (1993–2000), now at St Barnabas, Cambridge, and a wife and mum.

Student work in recent years

The ministry of looking after students today remains a very encouraging one. Each year, about a hundred students leave St Andrew the Great for God's wider harvest field. Of these, typically about twenty were not professing faith when they came up; about twenty will move immediately to the Far East or continental Europe; and a further twenty will go straight into paid Christian work. Of course, sadly, a number will also drift from Christ, which is as painful as it is inevitable. But I like what Simon Scott, who was the Students' Curate before me, has written: 'Every now and then I bump into someone who came to follow Christ while a student in Cambridge. They are now actuaries or teaching classics in a secondary school or working in the jewellery industry, standing up for Christ in often challenging circumstances.' We are blessed to have the opportunity and resources to be a significant help to students in their walk with Jesus through university, and naturally we try to make the most of it.

Aims and priorities

Our motto is Colossians 1:28–29, 'We proclaim him, admonishing and teaching everyone with all wisdom, so that we may present everyone perfect in Christ. To this end I labour, struggling with all his energy...' From this verse we derive four things to which we want to be committed.

The first is a *simple gospel* – 'We proclaim him'. Our aim is to teach Christ and to unite around him. We want to give students core gospel convictions, that they might stand on them and be unashamed of them. But it is not our aim for students to leave with firm opinions on secondary issues. As Mark Ashton used to say about Baptism and the Lord's Supper: 'Jesus told us to do them, and we've been arguing about them ever since!'

Our second commitment is to the *Bible* – 'admonishing and teaching everyone with all wisdom'. We believe that students will grow as they are taught the Bible, and therefore we run several meetings to provide a context for that:

- Sunday services, with expository preaching at their heart, and lasting only an hour to make it easy for students to bring friends.
- Student lunches afterwards, with topical talks to show how the Bible applies to all areas of life, and where students can ask their questions.
- Mid-week Bible studies, equipping students to read the Bible for themselves and teach it to others.
- Groups for those who are not Christians, or are very young Christians, with a Bible talk and then discussion sitting around tables.

Thirdly, we want to be committed to the *individual* – 'so that we may present everyone perfect in Christ'. It was the heart of Mark Ruston's ministry to meet individually with students each week, and it remains *the* major plank of the student ministry – the chief difference being that we are able to offer this kind of attention to many more undergraduates. In order to facilitate personal work on a wide scale, we have developed various strategies:

- The Jesus Lane Trust enables St Andrew the Great to employ up to six student workers each year.

- About forty-five members of the congregation lead the mid-week Bible studies, in order to get to know students through them.

- In the vacations we serve alongside students on summer ventures for teenagers, and also lead 'reading weeks' for students, where a party of between eight and twelve of us can read Christian books and listen to sermons together.

- Our student house party at Easter is often a timely opportunity for students to talk with an older Christian about life.

Our final commitment is to *prayer* – 'struggling with all [God's] energy'. That is obviously the case for the student staff: if any student visits us, we will pray for them by name until we know that they have either left Cambridge or settled at another church. But the student work is also the focus of the prayers of the whole church family, and is supported by many others through the newsletter for the Jesus Lane Trust.

I hope it is clear that the student ministry today is essentially just what it was fifty years ago. However, we do lay on more meetings than in the past, and perhaps some will wonder whether these activities undermine the work of the CICCU (Cambridge Inter-Collegiate Christian Union). Certainly I would hope not: I would stop them if I thought they did. The reason we run all these things, though, is that we believe that students are going to be more effective at living and speaking for Christ if they are discipled by older believers – and the biblically normal way of achieving that is through the local church. It seems to me to be no coincidence that so much of CICCU's leadership, year-on-year, is provided by those with whom we have been studying the Bible.

Changing times

The move to St Andrew the Great made many new things possible in terms of our care for students. But it is not merely the Round Church that has changed over the years – the whole university has. The proportions of male and independently educated students have gone down; the proportions of overseas and graduate students have gone up; a student is typically more invested in his or her studies (in all sorts of ways): social units, faculties and societies are becoming as important as colleges; the online, digital age has meant that students are less likely to turn out for evening talks or debates; and an aggressively pluralistic culture has brought us to the point where even the deans of colleges are forbidding students from handing out gospels.

These are significant challenges, to which we have only begun to respond. But it is still the case that students have rare opportunities. Perhaps their greatest gift is time. It would be pretty odd for most of us to go to a Christian meeting six days a week, but students can do it without any great cost to friendships in college or attention to their studies. And it is astonishing how fast a Cambridge student can grow in their knowledge and attitudes.

A second gift students have is flexibility. For the first time in their life, they find themselves with the freedom to take responsibility and make decisions, and, unlike the rest of us, they do not have the juggernaut of career and mortgage and children to turn around. So students not only learn but can change very quickly.

A third gift is the opportunity to try gospel ministry. Undergraduates have energy, creativity and initiative in spades; and it is wonderful to see these turned to service of Christ. A student will not be involved at St Andrew the Great for long before they are encouraged into leadership of some sort; for example, accepting the CICCU's invitation to become a college Christian Union leader, serving on Exec (the leadership committee), running a Christianity Explored course or some Bible studies in their college, helping on a Christian summer venture for teenagers, studying the Bible one-to-one with an unbeliever or preaching in a prison. Getting a taste of gospel ministry is very often life-changing for them.

One of our axioms is that we do not want the students serving the church itself. We could easily tie students up with leading our children's and youth groups, or helping with the cleaning or the bookstall or even leading our own mid-week Bible studies for students. But we prefer to set the students free to serve outside the church, making the most of the unique opportunities they have for sharing Christ with people they know from their college or sports team or university faculty or school – people whom the church could not so easily reach. In Acts, the accusation was made against the apostles that 'you have filled Jerusalem with your teaching' (Acts 5:28). Our role at St Andrew the Great is to encourage and equip the students to do something similar in Cambridge, and then to continue in this work wherever they go on to next.

Brian Elfick started running the student work at StAG in 2005 and was Students' Curate (2006-12).

I came up to Cambridge from a non-Christian home in Newcastle and in my first year I lived with sixteen others on S-staircase in Clare College including two Christians, Jonnie and Tom. Living alongside them, I saw that they were not living for the same things that I was. As they told me about Jesus, God began to convict me of my guilt before him, leading me to read John's gospel where I came to meet Jesus and grasp his death in my place on the cross. Not long after the beginning of the third term of my first year, I prayed with Jonnie that Jesus would be my Lord and Saviour.

After my conversion God continued to use them to disciple me. Early on, they helped me get into the habit of daily Bible reading and prayer and get stuck into St Andrew the Great and the Cambridge Inter-Collegiate Christian Union. I am grateful to church for the faithful Bible teaching, warm fellowship and opportunities to serve that it gave me.

Jonny Lee, member of StAG (2006–09), on the staff as Church Assistant (2009–10), pastoral assistant at Holy Redeemer, Streatham Vale, London.

I consider deciding to go to StAG as the best decision I ever made. (This may raise a few eyebrows, but I cannot remember back to when I became a Christian!). Under God I feel I owe almost everything to the ministry at StAG under Mark Ashton's leadership and am so very grateful.

I arrived in Cambridge as a Christian, but a pretty immature and clueless one. My life was following a fairly well-worn trajectory lacking biblical priorities or a passion for Christ. For example, I was headed towards law in the City because, well, that's what people did after a History degree at Cambridge.

All that changed thanks to my three years at StAG. While there, many people poured Bible teaching, time, energy, attention, love and prayer into my life. I learnt radical whole life discipleship. Before, I'd been coasting along, not taking my faith too seriously, then I suddenly found it impacting on parts of my life I thought had nothing to do with Jesus. I also began to have a desire to give Jesus all I had rather than just what was left over from the rest of my life. I might still end up doing City law

> but now the heart behind that would be so different. *That change of heart came by sitting under God's word in services, Focus, Student lunch and one-to-one Bible studies. My knowledge grew so much in such a short space of time and, thanks to the Holy Spirit, so did my love of Jesus in response.*
>
> *I'd wanted to go to Cambridge for years before I finally arrived there. But in the end it was mainly wonderful because of all God did in my life there, primarily through the ministry at StAG.*
>
> Alice Beckett (née Bagnall), undergraduate at StAG (2006–09), apprentice with Grace Church and 4 O'Clock Church, congregations of St Nicholas Church, Sevenoaks.

Endnotes

1. Watson, David. *My God is Real*, 1971.

CHAPTER 7

Serving an academic community
– 'town and gown'

Bob White

Families are perhaps the most wonderful, difficult, joyful, stressful, supportive, frustrating, emotional, loving forms of community life known to humankind. None of us chooses or can change our natural family members. Likewise, all Christians are children of the same heavenly Father and belong to the same family, yet in no way choose their fellow family members. Christian family life often mirrors many of the blessings and pains of normal family life.

Just like human families, each fellowship and congregation has its own particular make-up and idiosyncrasies while remaining part of the church universal. It is the task of the local church to reach out and to minister to those around it, in the particular circumstances in which it finds itself. For the Round Church/St Andrew the Great (StAG), one of the defining characteristics of its setting is the presence in the city of two universities and numerous colleges, English language schools, boarding schools and other educational establishments, together with many high-tech industries. The other characteristic is the extreme smallness of the resident population in the parish itself – a few dozen at most.

The same...

How should this academic setting change the ministry? Well, in one way, not at all. The greatest need of every person is to hear the gospel, to repent and to follow Jesus. And then to love him with all their heart and soul and mind. As a former Warden of Tyndale House, Bruce Winter, once commented in his earthy Australian way, 'we are all the same in the shower'. The preaching under both Marks was always centred on expounding and applying Scripture, usually by working through one of the books of the Bible. That is the primary way of teaching and of challenging both those who are already Christians and those who are not, whether they are academics or not.

...but different

Yet there are some special factors in a city such as Cambridge which is full of students. The most obvious is that many of the people both in the city and in church on a Sunday are transient. Folk are continually moving through, frequently on a three-year cycle, but often for much shorter periods if they are post-doctoral researchers or academics on sabbaticals. Many members of the congregation will spend a maximum of only a few dozen Sundays in church during their entire time in Cambridge. Allied to this, students arriving in Cambridge are often unchurched, with little understanding culturally of the Christian heritage. In previous generations, knowledge of basic Bible stories was common to practically everyone and could be taken for granted.

Compared with many local churches, the number of new Christians, and indeed of non-believers, in services week by week is very large. So this puts a premium on explaining the basic tenets of the gospel and of the Christian faith year after year. That does not mean that the preaching has to be repetitive, and certainly not narrow, since one way or another practically all of Scripture points to Jesus and to God's purposes for humankind. But it does put a premium on consciously and continually preaching the gospel: in fact, not a bad plan for any church.

The core congregation

But behind the large and transient congregation is a small but crucial core fellowship. They are there year-round and, by and large, they are also the main funders of the church work since students generally do not have a lot of money. They bring stability and continuity to the fellowship. They also bring numerous children since many are young professionals at that stage of their family life. Both Marks devoted the bulk of their ministry to one place, pastoring this one church. I well remember Mark Ashton commenting soon after he arrived that it is relatively easy to breeze in and then to leave after a few years. But if you are in it for the long haul, then building and maintaining relationships through all the ups and downs of church family life is what will show the distinctiveness of the Christian way.

Serving an academic community

What about the particular aspect of catering for academics? Church warden Stephen Oakley comments that 'Mark Ashton was absolutely right not to respect learning for its own sake.' But nonetheless, Mark Ashton had a deep desire to bring the abilities and skills of everyone, including academics, into the service of God. He started an annual dinner for senior members of the university – those with permanent or long-term jobs in the university such as lecturers and professors. The main aim was simply to bring academics together to hear a short talk, to eat together and to share news and pray together. Scholarship can be a lonely, isolated activity (as indeed the writer of Ecclesiastes recognised). Simply getting to know other Christians so that you recognise them as you pass in the street or the common room and to discover that many of the pressures you face are shared by others, is an immensely valuable and encouraging experience. Of course, that is a lesson that translates to other groups of people within churches with common occupations, be they stockbrokers, shop assistants, farmers, factory workers, teachers, carers, home-makers or whatever they may be.

Science and humanities

Another possibly surprising aspect of the church in Cambridge is that the great majority of students and academics are from science subjects rather than from the humanities. Far from the common misconception that science and Christian faith are somehow at loggerheads, the fact is that many scientists find their Christian faith to be completely coherent with their scientific work; that one supports the other. It is not surprising really: both science and Christianity believe in the concept of truth – that some things are right and others demonstrably wrong; both look for evidence and base conclusions on that; both believe that there is a profound reality behind the things we see and measure with our senses; both assume that there is an underlying consistency to the universe. For the Christian it is hardly surprising: we worship a consistent, loving, creator God – and scientists have the privilege of studying his creation as part of their day job. All of this may come as a surprise to those who are bombarded by media stories of the conflict between science and faith – stories that are often driven more by the media's need to fill headlines by highlighting disagreements than by reporting the more boring agreements of the majority.

For Mark Ashton, however, the humanities were always near to his heart and he longed to recapture them for Christ too. As Sujit Sivasundaram describes below, Mark took the initiative to start a reading group for those in the humanities. If Christians are to make a difference in the public square, they need to take all such opportunities to engage with contemporary thinking, be it at an academic level, or in politics, business, finance, sport, the caring professions or a wide range of other activities in our culture. Academia is an obvious and important constituency in the Cambridge context, but churches elsewhere will have equally pressing priorities they need to develop in different areas.

Christian fellowship

One of the enduring features of all Christian life – whatever the particular local setting – is that the people with whom we find ourselves sharing a common church life are not those we would necessarily choose to socialise with, to share our time and possessions with, or to labour alongside. That is one of the glories of the Christian family. One of the most practical marks of redeemed people is that they share fellowship with those who are, humanly speaking, poles apart. It is a sign of the reality of the new creation breaking into this one.

For example, it always amused us that Mark Ruston purposefully placed David C. C. Watson and his wife Loraine in the small Bible study group that met weekly in our home. David was a young earth creationist who wrote one of the most eloquent books of his time about it. Apart from anything else, I admired hugely his title *The Great Brain Robbery*. Naturally speaking, I am at the other end of the spectrum from him, believing that the best explanation we have of *how* God created this world in which we live is our scientific understanding of the evolutionary development of a universe of immense age. (In passing, it is worth noting that science can never provide meanings, or the *why* of our existence: for that we need revelation, which of course he has provided through Scripture and, supremely, through his Son, Jesus.) David and Loraine became dear friends and we shared much Christian study, prayer and fun together – though he never gave up trying to convert me to his way of thinking about the age of the Earth!

'Town and gown' is the particular setting of the church which the two Marks pastored. But there are lessons and values which are applicable to all Christian fellowships wherever they are: how a church is led, how to encourage folk to bring all their human endeavour under the Lordship of Christ, how to teach a diverse and often opinionated congregation to live together and how to model the love and self-giving service of the Christian family.

Robert (Bob) White was a member of the Round/StAG (1971–97). In 1997, he moved with other members of StAG to All Saints, Little Shelford. He is Professor of Geophysics at Cambridge University.

At the door of St Andrew the Great: a firm handshake, a wide smile and then the rather unexpected fact that he recalled my long Sri Lankan name, having met me just once before. This must be one of my first memories of Mark Ashton. Yet it is a telling one. For his was a ministry to real people. I arrived at St Andrew the Great as an international undergraduate student and was a member for fifteen years, before joining the congregation at St Matthew's, Cambridge. I now lecture at Cambridge University in the History Faculty.

Mark had an especial passion for the humanities, which came from his own degree in English. He loved making fun of scientists and engineers, and rather proudly announced that almost every one of his staff members had been arts students. But beside this typical banter, he was unusual in using poetry and philosophy in sermons, in order to engage with those from the arts. He was determined about the relevance of this, even though it was often critiqued at the weekly service planning meetings. When I gave him a book on post-modern theory, I was rather surprised to find a sermon serving as a direct response to it.

In his last years, Mark Ashton felt he wished to restore a Christian witness in the humanities, and established a reading group for those of us in this area. This is just one aspect of a wider vision which he cherished of capturing the university community for Christ, encompassing everyone from the new student to the most senior professor. The humanities continue to be a barren ground for the church, and Mark's vision is one we now should seek to follow. His challenge in this respect is to present the gospel clearly, attractively and boldly, even to the arts, which must be one of the most sceptical audiences of our present culture.

Sujit Sivasundaram, at StAG as undergraduate and postgraduate (1994–2001), lecturer in World History at Cambridge University and member of St Matthew's, Cambridge since 2009.

Mark Ruston was chaplain of my college (Jesus) in my final year as an undergraduate (1951 to 1952) and he came to know me through my being a member of the college Christian Union group. When I left Cambridge we lost touch. However, eighteen years later, when he was well established as vicar of the Round Church, he read of my appointment to a Lectureship in the university and wrote to me most warmly, inviting us as a family to consider the possibility of joining the congregation. We had personal links with members of some other churches but the work among sixth formers at the Round seemed a significant bonus for our stage of family life – so we joined the Round. We look back with deep thankfulness to God for Mark Ruston's pastoral initiative in 1970 and for the outstanding ministry of both Marks over the last fifty years.

Robin and Marian Porter Goff have been members of the Round/StAG since 1970. Robin was a University Lecturer in Engineering and a Fellow and Director of Studies at Fitzwilliam College. Now, in retirement, he is a Life Fellow of Fitzwilliam; Marian has run women's Bible studies for many years.

CHAPTER 8

Serving international visitors

Steve & Katie Tuck

I still remember the first proper conversation I had with Mark Ashton early in 1995. I had just come back from a couple of years abroad, and although I'd joined a vibrant church there, I had felt somewhat surplus to requirements and frankly, a foreigner. I remember the conversation well because much of it was surprising. To start with, it was a (very nice) surprise to be invited to the vicarage within days of returning, by a vicar I didn't really know. I had expected Mark would want to hear some gripping stories about foreign adventures. But no, after about thirty seconds of pleasantries, he asked where I wanted to serve in the church, and after a few minutes more, he suggested serving as part of an international student team, which was odd because St Andrew the Great didn't actually have any international students, let alone a team to serve them.

Early days

Or rather it would have been odd, except that it revealed Mark Ashton's unswerving view that it is God who builds his church. He explained that he had long wanted the church to serve foreigners. His previous work had been with people from different cultures, and he missed the mix. But more importantly, he reckoned the church at that time was poor at welcoming those in need and who looked different, so he hoped that welcoming people of different cultures might bring wider benefits. He had been praying that the church could serve international students since he had arrived five or six years before. I remember thinking then, if it was such a priority, why hadn't he done something? I realise now, of course, that he had.

What the ministry looked like, though, or what size it was, didn't seem to matter too much. I don't think he ever asked about the super welcome programmes that we cooked up (that were often anything but). Personalities didn't seem to matter, either. Mark Ashton was very keen to make sure people served, yes. But when we requested that 'impressive so and so' join the international student team, he often said no, and suggested that 'rather odd so and so' join instead. He explained, once, with a twinkle in his eye, that rather odd people tended to be well suited to working with people from other cultures. If God wanted it to happen, it would happen.

Prayer and unity

Mark Ashton's early advice had nothing to do with international ministry specifically. He simply stressed two things: prayer and unity. To take prayer first. When we first created the team, he said not to call a meeting for people who might be interested in international work, but to call a prayer meeting for it, preferably at an inconvenient time before the morning service. Three people turned up – two became stalwart, selfless members of that very first three-person team. The other, who already ran a home group, was ever supportive thereafter. The importance of unity was less obvious, thankfully, because it never became an issue. Mark Ashton warned that the chief danger to the international student work might be rivalry with the regular student work. Maybe because of that warning, it never happened.

Priorities

As for what the team got up to, that was left to us. Looking back, it was shaped by principles from the pulpit. High on the list was getting the team to serve others in response to what Christ had done for us. For example, team members committed to Sunday morning service attendance would wait at the door for the foreigner who usually turned up early or late, then sit with them, explain everything, and offer a lunch afterwards – almost always accepted gratefully. This meant putting some extra chicken in the pot, but it usually got eaten during Sunday afternoons. Many were the potential team members who feared missing time with their friends on a Sunday. Many were the actual team members who found new, rich friendships (and, of course, were able to include old friends, too).

Mark Ashton was keen that international student ministry happened in the local church, where possible, rather than be left outside it. He thought it good for the church and good for the students. We came to see the wisdom of that time and again: when overseas students found comfort from young and old in cold and lonely England; when they, in turn, were able to serve people in other walks of life; when they heard clear Bible teaching; and when church regulars who might never meet an overseas student in their normal course of life gave time, prayer and money to supporting the work.

How?

The man who had faithfully overseen international student work in Cambridge for many years, Bartow Wylie, suggested that we concentrate on the following, in this order:

1) making the church international-friendly

2) building up overseas Christians

3) explaining the gospel to the overseas unchurched

We hadn't really thought about making the church 'international-friendly', but we came to see the wisdom of Bartow's advice. We thank God for Mark Ashton's leadership in all of this. He made a point – every single week – of especially welcoming people from abroad. It sounds like a small thing, but it sent an important signal to visitor and regular alike. He quickly made sure overseas members were involved in upfront roles – reading the Bible, leading the prayers and so on. He welcomed feedback on sermons to make sure illustrations were global – out went references to British TV, in came international stories. He was happy for translations of the Bible passage to be given out ahead of the sermon, and for a special simple English group to meet as part of 'Christianity Explored' evenings.

And he gave international student work a central place in the church's monthly prayer meeting, even at the earliest stages. Looking back, however, the memory I cherish most was our first Christmas day at StAG – a turkey lunch, the Queen's speech on widescreen, fun and games for anyone with no home to go to. About eighty or so turned up that day, including Mark and Fiona dropping in for an hour or so, and just joining a group at a table and chatting away.

Mark Ashton also put the resources of the church behind the work. The team soon had a dozen or so members. The staff gave their time, the student curate spoke on our weekend away and Mark Ashton was always willing to speak at our get-togethers. Mark also told us that the church would underwrite our first weekend away. The break-even cost was something like £80 per person for the weekend, but he said it would be fine to say 'if you can't pay the full amount, pay what you can.' What we hadn't realised was that virtually no-one could afford more than a token amount. So when some eighty people came along, we found ourselves a few thousand pounds short. (Mark's support notwithstanding, my wife was rather nervous the following Monday about how the church manager, John Rose, would respond to news of such a shortfall. As it happened, a few days earlier, an anonymous gift for the weekend away had been sent in, for a little more than the shortfall.)

Making the church 'international-friendly' soon meant many overseas Christians came through the doors. For many in the congregation, Sunday morning became the most multicultural moment of the week. As these visitors became integrated – became church family – and as they were taught and encouraged in their faith, they usually brought friends from their home countries. Meanwhile the arrival of so many from abroad prompted more regular church members to get involved in international work, which in turn led to more help for the graduate groups and language students in town.

StAG experienced quite a culture shift in those days. But actually, it was in keeping with the church's historic mission to a university town which was changing fast. By the end of the century, nearly one in three students was a graduate, and half of those were from overseas. So reaching the university now meant reaching the overseas graduate students and the ever growing numbers of overseas undergraduates and language students on courses from two weeks to a year.

Moving forward

As for the team, that grew in size, got involved in more areas of church life and came to be led by full-time staff workers: first Caroline Rendle, then Sujit Sivasundaram, then an associate vicar, James Poole with two full-time assistants. I'm sure each of those folk could write much longer chapters than this one on the early development of the work. Looking at StAG's website ahead of writing this chapter, I was delighted to see all the wonderful things that seem to be happening now, and to read that StAG is an 'evangelical church in Cambridge city centre with a particular focus on students and internationals.' Quite a transformation. We thank God for Mark Ashton's vision for an international ministry in a local church, and his leadership in challenging the customs of the (hitherto very British) church to bring it about. We thank God too for giving us a pastor who took such tender care of us.

Stephen Tuck was a member of the Round/StAG (1989–2002) and is now teaching at Oxford University. Katie Tuck (née Newton) was an undergraduate and parish assistant (1992–2002) at StAG and is now a wife and mum. They are now members of St Ebbe's, Oxford.

I moved to Cambridge from Nigeria in October 1992 to pursue my MPhil/ PhD at Trinity College. Initially, I attended a different church but in 1994, Steve Tuck, a friend of mine who was also at Trinity College at the time, introduced me to StAG. Steve was involved with outreach for international students at StAG. The friendship and fellowship at StAG made me feel at home immediately. After my PhD in 1996, I stayed on as a Research Fellow at Trinity College. I was involved together with Abraham and Ruth Folayan, fellow StAG members, in leading the African Christian Fellowship in Cambridge. Mark Ashton's practical teachings at StAG equipped and helped me tremendously during my stay in Cambridge.

In January 1999, I married Folake and she also joined StAG. We both have good memories of our time at StAG. My favourite song in church then was 'Jesus' love is very wonderful'. Our faith, however, was tested about a year into our marriage when our first child was still-born after full term. It was a devastating experience. The doctors at Addenbrooke's Hospital could not find the cause of death. Being away from Nigeria with no family support in Cambridge, friends and staff at StAG supported us through prayers, visits and making sure we were fine. Mark Ashton wrote us a letter assuring us of the prayers of the church, love and sympathy. I quote a part of his letter: 'I know it must be so hard for you to bear such an awful personal tragedy when you are so far away from your own families. A church family in a different culture will only be a very feeble substitute, but we do feel for you and we pray that God will comfort you Himself, as the One who has conquered death and shared every grief and burden of the human heart.'

…We really thank the church family for demonstrating the love of God to us in practical ways. We moved to Singapore in 2000 and have since been blessed with three wonderful children named Mofopefolu ('I offer thanks to God'), Obaloluwa ('The Lord is King') and Ajiboluwa ('Born unto the Lord').

Adekunle Adeyeye, member of StAG (1992–2000), now teaching at the National University of Singapore, and a member of Grace Assembly of God, Singapore.

Chapter 9

Serving the local community
– parents and toddlers

Elizabeth Waldock

Small beginnings

When Mark and Fiona arrived in Cambridge in 1987, they were asked by the church to build up the work among families but not at the expense of the student work. In their previous church in Balham, Fiona had set up a mums and pre-school group called *Chatterbox* which had been effective in drawing local families into the church. It was with this vision that a baby and toddler group, run by Fiona, was started in the sitting room of the Round Church vicarage – with some church mums, their babies and toddlers, and some of their friends and neighbours. It was known as *Bouncers*.

After two years it outgrew the vicarage and moved next door into a college common room until 1994, when the group transferred to the newly refurbished St Andrew the Great building (StAG) and became known as Bounce-A-Round. Though the venue changed, the purpose of the group remained the same – to act as a springboard or launch-pad into the life of the church for those who came along; not simply one more parents and toddlers group but rather a place where parents and carers could meet and make friends with local Christians and thus be given the chance to consider Christ and his gospel.

The format remained largely the same – two hours of mid-morning play for children, time to chat for the adults, singing, craft-making, story reading and refreshments. Within a short time the group had grown to take over the whole auditorium of the church (transformed each Wednesday morning by hard-working parish assistants and other helpers).

Priorities

Humanly speaking, Bounce-A-Round always depended on a core of committed church mums and other church members to run effectively. Fiona would say that, periodically, the group needed to reassess and re-evaluate its priorities. Over time these priorities came to be expressed in the following terms: in-reach, out-reach and internationals.

In-reach: A group such as Bounce-A-Round provides a natural context for friendships to develop among church mums (something not easily achieved through attending church services alone), with an opportunity for them to give and receive support and encouragement, both spiritually and practically. That support comes in many different guises – sometimes a 'word in season' or simply a listening ear at a difficult time. Many have grown spiritually through helping to lead a Christianity Explored course with another member of the team, or from the discussions at the 'in-reach' evenings. Practically speaking, it was often a case of home-cooked meals following the birth of a new baby. Motherhood is often a time of immense change and many church mums appreciated the support, encouragement and training they received through Bounce-A-Round, and the chance to serve in a new way.

Out-reach: Bounce-A-Round always aimed to be open and active in welcoming non-church parents and carers. Soon large numbers of children and their parents or carers were attending regularly, many of whom would not otherwise have found themselves in a church building. Often they continued to come over a period of many years, returning to be part of the group with successive children. Partly because of the nature of Cambridge as a city, Bounce-A-Round has always been a wonderfully diverse group – both socially and culturally. A New Zealander, Anne-Marie, expresses it like this, 'It brought together parents and carers from all walks of life – culturally, economically and educationally. What forged our friendships was a cuppa, chat and mutual support.'

One of the main tools for 'out-reach' was the parent-friendly evening events which developed over the years. These 'Curry & Childcare' evenings consisted of a curry and a talk on a relevant issue such as 'Emergency First Aid for under-fives' or 'Behaviour Management (Toddler Taming!)'. These 'link events' were not usually evangelistic but the speaker was always a Christian and the talk usually involved an element of testimony and a weaving in of the relevance of Christian belief. They were a particularly good time for the mums (or dads) who come to Bounce-A-Round midweek to bring their partner along to meet the other parents. Christmas and summer lunches for over 100 were often held following family-friendly services; these are for the whole family, with the aim of sharing lives and the gospel. Many of the Bounce-A-Round families who came would not normally attend church on Sunday. When further interest was expressed, there was the opportunity to attend a daytime Christianity Explored course, either one-to-one or in a group.

Sometimes it is the dad who is the principal carer on a Wednesday and, for a number of men, Bounce-A-Round provided opportunities for them to build friendships with other dads. Some would say that men are naturally less talkative than women so it can take longer to build friendships, but friendships have grown and this led to whole families coming to services and starting to become involved in the life of the church.

One mum describes how she heard about the Christianity Explored course through her husband because of his attendance at Bounce-A-Round. They went to a Curry & Childcare meal together where the speaker addressed the topic of Emergency First Aid. Sarah says, 'On a practical level this event was really helpful in terms of what was shared medically, but what struck me about this lady was that she was utterly convinced that her prayers and faith would help them all.' Sarah went on to do a Christianity Explored course and speaks of how 'my understanding of and relationship with Jesus was changing from a theoretical to a personal one. Since then I have been attending StAG on Sundays with the children, joined a Bible study group while on maternity leave, and have now joined a new home group.'

Internationals: A significant number of those coming to Bounce-A-Round are from overseas and are often only passing through Cambridge for between one and three years, usually for the purpose of academic study. They are often older than British postgraduate students and often arrive already married and with children – or perhaps have children while they are here. Many of them speak limited English and have met few people outside the work environment. For some of the women it is their husbands who are studying and being away from home in an unfamiliar city can be a very lonely and isolating experience for them. For many Bounce-A-Round became a lifeline, meeting others in similar circumstances, making friends, practising English and receiving support in mothering. For those who are interested, the Bounce-A-Round team developed an 'orientation course', covering areas such as English culture, culture shock, education, health systems, cookery, etc. The idea was that the international mums from the church family could bring friends to it. Out of this, the opportunity was given to find out about Christianity through a Christianity Explored course in simple English, with support given by the international workers on the StAG staff team.

The team

The effectiveness, humanly speaking, of Bounce-A-Round in these three spiritual aims has always depended on the extent to which the vision was caught by the church families at Bounce-A-Round. The group needed to be 'owned' and run by mums from the church and a team of practical helpers. The practical helpers fulfilled a vital role, enabling the mums to concentrate on their children and to build friendships. On top of that, their willing service provided the visitors to Bounce-A-Round with a glimpse of life under the kingship of Jesus Christ, with all the setting up and clearing away, registering families on arrival and departure, providing refreshments and manning the messy play and crafts each week.

Mark Ashton always encouraged the team to see their service coming not out of obligation but out of gratitude for all that Christ and the gospel had given us. To keep this focus, the team prayed together each week before opening the doors and, as well as on-going, individual prayer over the term, there was a regular prayer meeting when the team prayed for each of the three areas of ministry.

Issues

A group such as this changes and evolves, and different issues present themselves from time to time. For Bounce-A-Round, one regular issue has been what to do about the large numbers attending. A wonderful 'problem' to have, of course! But it has always been important that Bounce-A-Round does not become so big numerically that the group strays beyond the reach of effective ministry. For reasons of safety and space, since moving to StAG, the number attending was limited to around seventy families at any one time. Various strategies were considered so that no-one had to be turned away from the group. Running an extra session on another morning was ruled out because of the lack of extra team members to set it up and run it. In 1999, it was decided to open the church for a longer period (9.45 a.m. to 1.45 p.m.), with parents and carers attending for a two-hour slot within that time. This meant that more families could be accommodated. It avoided huge queues at the door plus the possible disappointment of being turned away, as had been the case when Bounce-A-Round was open only for a couple of hours (10 a.m. to 12 p.m.). Timings are always under review.

Many people who are setting up or running a similar group in their church will debate whether or not to have any overt Christian content during the session, through Bible stories and Christian songs. In the early days, the Bounce-A-Round team decided that there would not be any formal Christian content during the sessions and that the Christian gospel would be presented through individual conversations and through inviting people to the 'link events'. So the story was just a story, not a Bible story, and the songs were along the lines of the ever popular 'Sleeping Bunnies' rather than Christian songs. The team wanted to make it as easy as possible for those who weren't Christians to come along and to feel unpressurised while they were there. Having said that, any visitors to Bounce-A-Round who expressed any interest in the gospel would find that there were plenty of Christian mums and dads who were more than delighted to chat about their faith and to point others to the Lord Jesus – and everyone was invited to and encouraged to attend the regular link events.

At other times, the team decided to introduce Christian songs and Bible stories, on the basis that gentle Christian content like this can set the tone for the session, mark the group out as different from other groups, give the children and parents a little taste of the gospel and perhaps provoke conversations. Whatever conclusion is reached, perhaps the key point is that the group is run by a committed group of Christian mums (and, from time to time, dads) who have a vision for reaching the local community with the gospel of Jesus Christ.

The story continues

As with all ministry, Bounce-A-Round is certainly not one big success story: there have been times of growth and encouragements, and other times when the work was tough-going and priorities had to be reassessed. Any 'successes' have come through prayer and by God's grace. But the ministry of Bounce-A-Round continues to flourish and we pray that, in his goodness, God would continue to use this group to build his church.

Elizabeth Waldock was a member of StAG (1997–2004) and moved in 2004 with other members of StAG to Christ Church, Cambridge. She is a wife and mum.

I first went to Bounce-A-Round on the recommendation of another new mum. What struck me immediately was the warm welcome I received. It was a fantastic place to meet other parents, there was an incredibly friendly atmosphere and plenty of activities for the children.

My eldest child was still a baby when I started going. I had been brought up in a Christian family but had stopped attending church in my late teens and had never made any firm commitment despite the encouragement of those around me. Having a child got me thinking about what I really believed and it is through Bounce-A-Round that I began to explore the possibility that the Christian message was true. The first step on my journey was to attend the family carol service – I still attended church at Christmas and Easter with my family so this wasn't too difficult. This led eventually to attending a Christianity Explained course and to making a commitment to follow Jesus.

I had a lot of fun at Bounce-A-Round, as did my children. Eventually I started to help out and to help lead the singing. My journey is on-going and has not always been easy, but the support I received in the early days at Bounce-A-Round and the friendships I made there helped carry me through. I can now see how God was at work in my life. Most notably he brought me into contact with lots of Christians and showed me that there was something 'different' about them.

Nicola Hamill-Stewart, member of StAG (1998–2008), then moved in 2008 with other members of StAG to St Matthew's, Cambridge, part-time librarian, wife and mum.

Chapter 10

Serving the local area – church plants and grafts

Christopher Ash

What does a city-centre church do when God blesses the ministry and gives growth? Does it seek to grow further, maybe to become (in British terms) a *very* big city-centre church? The project to restore the St Andrew the Great building (StAG) for Christian use, as a fairly large and well-equipped city-centre building, is described in Chapter 5. This enabled the Round Church student work to thrive, supported by a growing and committed all-year-round 'heart'. But even before the church council agreed to go ahead with St Andrew the Great, church-planting was being discussed for the future. Could we resist the temptation to 'build church' for our own glory? Could we avoid becoming a magnet drawing keen Christians into the city centre and away from supporting faithful gospel ministry elsewhere in the city or in the surrounding villages? The church leadership decided at quite an early stage in the St Andrew the Great project that if God continued to bless the work, they would seek ways either to plant new churches or reinvigorate struggling ones.

The result so far, under God, has been the three church plants, to Little Shelford, to Christ Church and to St Matthew's. The details of these three stories would probably be of interest only to those involved in them. The first was to a village church, the second and third to city churches; but all three projects shared some characteristics that reflect the ministry vision of St Andrew the Great, and I hope it will be of wider interest to outline the salient points.

Dangers of bigger churches

One of the main reasons for pursuing the idea of planting was the perception that a bigger church is not necessarily a better church. A bigger church will be a better church if the growth is gospel growth, through conversion rather than just through the transfers of already-Christian people from other churches. A bigger church may be a useful church if its size is used to staff and resource a particular ministry, such as to students, and if it works proactively to train and send gospel workers out. But a bigger church can become something of an ego-trip for its staff and members, sometimes it does little more than suck already-Christian people away from more authentically local churches. They may just move because they like the good feelings and buzz that come from larger gatherings. There are ungodly reasons for wanting to belong to a bigger church, and ungodly reasons for wanting to be on the staff of one. We wanted to avoid these dangers and to be a city-centre church that serves and promotes the growth of other local churches. We wanted to multiply ministry and glorify Jesus Christ, not to magnify ourselves.

Bible teachers and Bible-taught

The second part of the vision was the very simple observation that at the heart of a local church is Bible teaching and preaching. This relates to the first three of Mark Ashton's eight convictions (Chapter 1). The word of God does the work of God through regular preaching and Bible teaching in the local church.

It follows that the relationship between the main Bible teacher and the members of the church is critical. Members of a church must trust the Bible teachers to be faithful and must be willing gladly to place themselves under that Bible-teaching ministry. (This is one reason why it does not work simply to suggest to church members that they move to any old struggling local church. They may have chosen to belong to the city-centre church precisely because they do not trust the Bible-teaching ministry in that other church!

Sheep will go where they find food, and it is good that they do.) So the plan was that a man should join the staff as one of the main Bible-teaching team and stay on staff for long enough to build up trust in his ministry. Only then would a group of church members gladly volunteer to go with him to a church plant. Incidentally, this makes the whole process a little nerve-wracking for the leaders; Frank Price, Steve Midgley and I had to commit to leading our respective plants before we knew for sure that anyone would trust us enough to volunteer to come with us!

Before, during and after the initiation of each project, the quality of trust and relationship between the leaders and the members was critical. Time invested in building those relationships was never wasted.

This conviction was the heartbeat of the church plants. Each of us tried to adapt to the different circumstances and histories of the three receiving churches. But the non-negotiable part is that the word of God does the work of God. It was this conviction also which energised the re-filling of St Andrew the Great after each plant.

Dependence on God in prayer

One of Mark Ashton's convictions – shared with others, of course – is that prayer lies at the heart of any local church. We firmly believed in this when embarking on the three Church Growth Initiatives. Long before settling on where to move, we began to pray together, to ask God to lead and guide us, and to open and close doors as he chose. The process of finding where to go, negotiating the agreements, deciding who would come, and actually launching out on each project, had to be soaked in prayer. These projects were a long way away from carefully and strategically planned initiatives, in which we might have asked God to rubber-stamp our tidy plans. At many times, those of us leading these plants felt completely at sea. Had it not been for the grace of God in answer to many prayers, we would have given up again and again.

Reclaiming lost ground

There are many different models for church-planting, and there are pros and cons of each. There is something rather simple, even sexy, about planting a church from scratch. Sometimes this is the best way – as, for example, where there has never been any sort of even approximate gospel witness in an area, or perhaps on a large estate. Often, however, there has been gospel witness in an area in years past, and the best thing we can do is to seek to reclaim lost ground by re-planting back into an existing church that has fallen on hard times. St Andrew the Great sought to do this within the structures of its own denomination, the Church of England. None of the Church Growth Initiatives would have gone ahead had it not been for the support of the Bishop and Diocesan authorities. We thank God for their encouragement and help.

This process of working within existing structures was much slower and more complicated than virgin church-planting but, in our social context, possibly more beneficial for the progress of the gospel. It was more complicated because it meant long and sensitive negotiations with the members and councils of the receiving churches. It meant bending over backwards not to be seen as imposing a takeover on any of these churches. Indeed, for each project, there were exploratory conversations with potential receiving churches that came to nothing because the suggested receiving church did not feel the project was appropriate for them. Frank Price withdrew from seven possible churches before St Matthew's opened up. This was entirely right. It meant that each project went ahead only when the members of the receiving church effectively issued an invitation and welcomed the project. We called the projects 'Church Growth Initiatives' to acknowledge the fact that each was an initiative to bring fresh life and growth into an existing church, rather than planting a church where there was none before. I remember vividly that Little Shelford was originally suggested to us by the Archdeacon, and that the project did not go ahead until the existing Little Shelford Church Council voted overwhelmingly in favour of inviting us to join them. None of the Church Growth Initiatives would have gone ahead without that kind of invitation.

No empire-building

We were very concerned that the church-planting projects should avoid any danger of magnifying St Andrew the Great. We saw that it is all too easy for an influential city-centre church to plant in such a way as effectively to increase its own sphere of influence, to build its empire by planting imperial outposts and to end up creating its own denomination. St Andrew the Great bent over backwards to avoid these dangers. From the moment the leaders and planting group were commissioned and sent, the apron strings were cut. Although there were countless ties of friendship and prayer, for which we all thank God, there were no formal ties. Steve, Frank and I ceased to be on the staff of St Andrew the Great from the first day of each of our plants.

This was not always understood, but it was very important. When we moved to Little Shelford in 1997, we faced the problem that we moved into a village with hardly any singles in their twenties or thirties or young marrieds without children, the groups who provided the bulk of the volunteer staffing for children's and youth work teams at St Andrew the Great. How were we to fill our children's and youth teams? The suggestion was made that some from those groups in St Andrew the Great might come out to run our groups on a Sunday morning, while remaining as members at St Andrew the Great and returning there on Sunday evening. After discussing this generous suggestion we decided against it. We wanted everyone who joined the plant to commit themselves one hundred percent to it and to cut all ties of church belonging to the sending church. This felt risky, but I think it was wise.

Yet part of the human dynamic of these kinds of projects is that the receiving church often perceives itself as the victim of a takeover bid from an 'imperial' city-centre church. It was therefore all the more important to make sure there was no truth in those myths that circulated so mischievously (as they did). The importance of building personal relationships of trust was paramount. A few of the Christ Church planting group began attending and helping with the evening service at Christ Church even before the plant project had been agreed. This was an example of sacrificial building up of trust. Each project took significant time to come to fruition. Moving to Little Shelford was like giving birth to an elephant, with a two-year gestation period. Christ Church took at least a year.

A few weeks after we began in Little Shelford, we received a generous cheque from the St Andrew the Great Gift Day. I telephoned to ask if there were any particular ways they would like us to use it, and was given the firm reply that this was entirely up to the Little Shelford Church Council, which at that early stage had only a very small minority of new members from the planting group.

They wanted quite simply to give the gift with no strings attached and to trust Little Shelford to use the money as we saw fit.

Generosity

This generous gift naturally leads into the fifth feature I want to highlight. The spirit that animated all three projects was one of overwhelming generosity, springing from the firm belief that the gospel is the instrument Jesus uses to build his church, and that generosity is intrinsic to authentic gospel living. At one level, each project was sheer costly loss to St Andrew the Great. Again and again, they gave not only a staff member or two (who are pretty easily replaceable) but a substantial slice of the very best and most committed long-term church members. In 1997 about fifty of us were sent to All Saints, Little Shelford. In 2004 a hundred or so were sent with Steve Midgley to Christ Church.[1] In 2008 a further hundred or so were sent with Frank Price to St Matthew's. These numbers were not set in advance. Mark Ashton and the leadership at St Andrew the Great encouraged all sorts of people to move, and set no cap on how many might decide to do so.

These groups included outstandingly mature men and women. Three of the couples who moved to Little Shelford had combined histories at the Round Church of about seventy-five years (roughly a quarter of a century for each couple). They included the Chairman of the St Andrew the Great Church Council. There were some singles who very bravely joined us, knowing full well that most people in the new church would be married. One couple moved to St Matthew's after forty years at the Round Church and St Andrew the Great. All these cut their ties with St Andrew the Great at very considerable emotional and personal cost to themselves, and also at great personal cost to St Andrew the Great.

In addition, every man and woman who moved to Little Shelford, Christ Church or St Matthew's also transferred their giving from the start. Each time this made a substantial hole in the St Andrew the Great finances. For example, the departure of the 2008 group to St Matthew's reduced the regular annual giving to St Andrew the Great by £100,000 overnight.

While this generous spirit was shown by St Andrew the Great as a whole, it reflected the gospel generosity of Mark Ashton particularly.

Mark repeatedly reminded St Andrew the Great that 'growth means change and change is often painful. We embrace the pain of change gladly for the sake of the gospel.' Not only did Mark repeatedly refuse offers of 'advancement' for himself, he also used to say that if St Andrew the Great were to fade away while the church plants prospered, it would be worth it, if that was God's plan.

There is no doubt that for St Andrew the Great being a sending church like this was pure loss. There was perhaps a certain sense of adventure and dependence upon God for those being sent out; there was nothing but a big painful hole for those left behind. No church will do this (and certainly not repeatedly) without the strong conviction, from the leadership to all the members, that God honours gospel generosity in all its forms. God has certainly honoured this repeated generosity, enabling St Andrew the Great to recover and rebuild both with people and with financial provision leading to continued fruitful ministry. Frank Price speaks of the (perhaps mythical) worm, each part of which regrows after the worm has been cut in half. It is a vivid image conveying something of the pain of the planting process.

All of us involved in these three planting endeavours thank God for the gospel generosity of Mark Ashton and St Andrew the Great under his leadership.

Christopher Ash was Families Curate at StAG (1993–97), then Rector of All Saints, Little Shelford (1997–2004). He is now Director of the PT Cornhill Training Course and a member of Emmanuel, Wimbledon.

In the twelve months before the graft to Christ Church, Mark Ashton would often speak in grave tones of the cost involved in a church plant. He would describe the impact on those leaving as well as the impact on those staying behind. I remember him saying that even though the two church buildings were less than a mile apart, relationships would never be the same again. After a while, I couldn't help thinking he was rather overstating the case.

Then our final Sunday at StAG arrived. Those leaving were invited to the front while those staying commissioned us for this new venture. And suddenly I could see what he had been talking about. Some of those standing at the front had become Christians at StAG and it had been their spiritual home for twenty years since. Now they were leaving. Others were leaving a church which contained some of their closest friends. I'd only been involved at StAG for three years, but the sense of loss was considerable. The friendships we develop with those we serve alongside in ministry are very special and it was sad to bring them to an end.

And Mark was right. Even though we were only a few hundred yards up the road, it was years before we saw many of those people again. Many friendships that were sustained by being part of the same fellowship and that relied on our Sunday meetings together were effectively coming to an end.

But that wasn't the only cost. By generously encouraging as many to leave as he could, Mark Ashton ensured that ninety or so adults moved to Christ Church. Almost all were right at the heart of things and gave generously in time and money. Their departure left large gaps in the ministry and the budget. This was something Mark Ashton positively welcomed. He was convinced that a church that is learning to be sacrificially generous (both of people and wealth) is a church that is learning to be shaped by the gospel. Because the gospel is about a God who gives everything for us, he wanted disciples and churches to do likewise and to learn to give without worrying about the cost. He was sure such an attitude would be to our spiritual profit. And when, not much more than a year later, we heard of numbers increasing and the holes we had left behind being filled, we knew he was right.

Steve Midgley, Associate Vicar at StAG (2001–04), now Minister of Christ Church, Cambridge.

What has been special about being part of the Christ Church 'graft'? A whole host of things spring to mind. For us personally, we think the best thing has been the opportunity to serve in practical and hopefully useful ways in areas which were not really possible before. Through our involvement in leading a home group together, helping with children's work and serving in church leadership, we have both been challenged and seen our faith grow. Christ Church has also proved to be a wonderful nurturing environment for our son to grow in faith himself, with marvellous caring leaders in the various groups. And it has all been based on thorough and relevant Bible teaching week by week. This has drawn people together into a loving, supportive church family, firmly founded on Christ and increasingly passionate about reaching the local community with the gospel.

David and Caroline Peet, members of StAG (1991–2004), David works at the Cavendish Laboratory, Cambridge University, Caroline is an Executive Head teacher; both joined Christ Church, with other members of StAG in 2004.

> *Mark Ashton told me when I started at StAG that the best way to make the graft happen was to preach the gospel faithfully and clearly, rather than to negotiate with other churches, come up with great ideas or win people over by persuasion. I keep reminding myself that only gospel preaching could account for the rapid growth at StAG in those four years after Steve Midgley took away so many. Some church leaders visited from Dublin and asked Mark Ashton, Steve Midgley and me, 'How on earth do you plant out two lots of a hundred people in under five years?' They took a lot of convincing that we didn't have any strategy, secrets, or special advantages. It happened because of the word of God doing its work.*

Frank Price, Associate Vicar for Families at StAG (2004–08), now Minister at St Matthew's Church, Cambridge.

Endnotes

1. Seventy-five adults and twenty-five children went from StAG to Christ Church, Cambridge.

CHAPTER 11

Serving the wider church

Robert Slipper, Abraham & Ruth Folayan, Nerena Nethercoat, Julian Hardyman, Sarah Collins, William Taylor & Bill Salier

This chapter draws together a number of examples of how St Andrew the Great (StAG) has been used by God to benefit the wider church, both in this country or overseas. In some cases, it has been through funding ministry in another church or in another part of the world; in other cases, through supporting, training and encouraging people who are in Cambridge for a short time and go on to serve the Lord elsewhere. The following contributions reflect on the question, how has StAG served the wider church?

Partnership in the gospel with a small, rural church

Soon after my arrival in the large Norfolk village of Terrington St Clement, I was approached by representatives from St Andrew the Great's church council about the possibility of StAG supporting us. StAG was looking to support a like-minded ministry elsewhere in the diocese of Ely, principally by funding (completely) a senior assistant member of staff. On the edge of The Wash, Terrington St Clement is as far away from Cambridge geographically as it is possible to get within the diocese – and a long way from Cambridge socially too. But the 'partnership in the gospel' that has built up has been of inestimable benefit to the church in Terrington – and,

I hope, for StAG too on the grounds that 'whoever sows generously will also reap generously' (2 Cor. 9:6).

Plans developed and a new trust was set up at the end of 2002 to fund the post for three years and to act as employer. Just a fortnight later, Dave Lewis arrived as 'Ministerial Assistant', and he and his wife Kate were with us for over four years. For two of those years, Dave was a part-time student on the Cornhill Training Course (a training course with a primary aim of training preachers), but the rest of his time was spent wholly within Terrington. He took over as the co-ordinator of our children's and youth work, with Sunday morning groups, introducing an annual holiday club (reaching 90% unchurched children), a small youth group and, in due course, a new after-school club. He also took an increasing role in the preaching ministry, in small group ministry (devising a discipleship course himself) and in pastoral ministry with a wide cross-section of the church family. After two years, some members of the Terrington Church family began to take a role in funding the post, but by far the greater part of the funding still came from StAG, who extended their initial gift.

It was a hard time for many of us after Dave left and I was back on my own, but StAG decided to keep supporting the ministry in Terrington. So, with folk in Terrington taking on a greater financial responsibility (and with the help of Christ Church, Cambridge, and a number of other trusts) I was able to seek another colleague; the following year I was joined by Chris Tinker and his wife Sophie. Chris took up where Dave had left off in leading the children's and youth department and added a new group for older children which met on a Sunday afternoon. He also pioneered and maintained our website, developed a full preaching and pastoral schedule and, as an ordained person, soon started helping with weddings and funerals.

The link with StAG has meant the two churches regularly praying for each other, and a number of visits between the two congregations. Members of the church in Terrington were delighted when invited to come to Cambridge for a day out – the highlight of which was joining the folk at StAG for a sumptuous tea and the evening service. And the visits of the Trustees and other members of StAG to Terrington have become special annual events. Moreover, StAG also gave a significant gift for Terrington's development project, helping to provide toilets and a servery.

The impact of StAG's support has been enormous. It has meant that the church in Terrington has been able to reach out with the gospel far more than would otherwise have been the case. It has meant that we have been able to maintain and even to expand significantly our work with children and young people in a district where few churches have any such ministry at all. It has given the Christians (and others) of Terrington a whole new experience of Christian fellowship. It has meant that I have been able to do more than simply keep the show on the road, which is so often the *best* for which the rural minister can hope; and the fact that we have thus been able to provide a *gospel* ministry has meant that it is both proper and wise for me to continue there. It has meant that I have had a colleague and friend with whom to share the ups and downs of ministry, making continuing at Terrington not just feasible but a privilege for which I am very grateful personally.

StAG has already shown a more than six-figure financial commitment to this small, local – some might say 'non-strategic' – body of Christians, and a prayer commitment which cannot be measured. It already overflows in 'many expressions of thanks to God' and has changed lives for eternity. Thank you, Lord – and thank you, StAG.

Robert Slipper was an undergraduate at the Round (1984–87). He is now Vicar of Terrington St Clement.

*****

Partnership in the gospel overseas

Our initial contact with StAG dates from when my wife Ruth and I came from our home country of Nigeria as 'mature' students to study at Romsey House, one of Cambridge's theological training colleges. I had one year of part-time practical attachment with the Round Church on the invitation of Mark Ashton. He asked me to initiate some ministry to overseas students attending the Round – West Africans, Chinese, and Americans. Ken Webster (then Church Manager) was already ministering to Japanese students and we worked together. When Mark Ashton gave you a job to do, he expected you to do it, encouraged you at it and impressed on you the importance of prayer. He invited about five of us (all over fifty years old) to meet with him weekly for prayer, not only for our various ministries but for the whole church. Mark had a tremendous gift for remembering names. I later realised that you remember those for whom you pray often. That was Mark Ashton! (John 10:14ff)

The move from the Round to St Andrew the Great demonstrated Mark Ashton's exemplary leadership quality. As he said in the church magazine: 'Many of us have been put to the test by the St Andrew the Great project in trusting God with our finances in a way we have never done before.' For him, the huge investment in the rebuilding project was for no other reason but the proclamation of the gospel. When StAG was opened in 1994, it was with a week-long mission, *Building for Life*, and giving for overseas mission continued throughout the project, alongside giving for the building. The support of missionaries was maintained and even expanded and, through the leadership of Mark Ashton, the Overseas Mission Group at StAG started to support our ministry in Malawi in 1995. Nothing must take away the centrality of the word from the church.

Mark Ashton asked people to work hard – and he was there to show what he meant. Many of us who saw him at work felt he probably worked himself a bit too hard! He was grateful to God for every opportunity to serve the cause of the gospel. And if you ask what makes ministry faithful and fruitful, we learn from Mark Ashton at least three things: recognising the importance of the word and of prayer; focus on the mission of the church; a people-oriented ministry that seeks the glory of God.

Abraham and Ruth Folayan were on placement at StAG (1993–94) while studying at Romsey House (theological training college), Cambridge. They were subsequently supported by StAG while Missionary Lecturers at the Evangelical Bible College of Malawi where Abraham was Principal. Now retired, they are back home at the Evangelical Church of West Africa, Lemu Road, Kaduna, Nigeria.

*****

Partnership in the gospel with individuals

'Not to us, O LORD, not to us, but to your name be the glory, because of your love and faithfulness.' (Ps. 115:1) That was the verse we looked at in my last meeting at the Overseas Mission Group at StAG. I had to leave the room while the group decided about the possibility of supporting and partnering me in going to work with students in Durban, South Africa, to teach the Bible. StAG has already provided an amazing five years of generous support for the work I am involved with on the university campuses in Durban and in helping at a regional Bible training course for local apprentices and others.

I was at St Andrew the Great for six years – first as a congregation member (with the 20s & 30s group) and then as a member of staff when I was involved mostly with student work. The friendships in the 20s & 30s group kept me persevering in a teaching qualification which otherwise I would never have finished and kept me putting my hope in our God who is always faithful. I joined the student team after that first year.

My time on the staff team was a great stretching, grounding and training time as I grew to feel even more part of the StAG family. Mark Ashton's weekly 'thoughts' from his Bible reading would challenge us. Student staff meetings were the training ground for thinking how to teach and care for the students. All the things I learnt with my team then have been invaluable for working with my present team. And all those mistakes.... what a gracious team I was working with!

Nerena Nethercoat was a member of StAG (2000–06) as a congregation member and on the staff as an apprentice. She is now at Christ Church, Glenwood in Durban, South Africa, working with women and students.

*****

Partnership in the gospel with other local ministers

I became a Christian on a teenage conference at which Mark Ashton was the main speaker. I was later to discover that he had been converted in the same place in Oxford, albeit a few years before. Then, as pastor of a nearby church, I found Mark the best of neighbours. He was particularly fine in a crisis. Eden suffered two during my time and in each Mark was quickly to the fore. One difficult autumn, Mark himself insisted on taking the Eden pulpit for a Sunday previously earmarked for a StAG colleague. Our administrator thought Mark would be too busy but he was obdurate that he was going to preach for us that Sunday. The gesture was greatly appreciated, as was the sermon. I am sure he was as busy as he could be, but supporting a fellow church in need mattered to him.

In more steady times, Mark would regularly take the initiative to get our staff teams together or to meet individually. He would seek me out, ply me with cake and quiz me hard. It took a while before I realised that if I didn't ask *him* questions, I would spend an hour listening to my own voice answering *his*! I find it hard to imagine he learned very much from me. For my part, I gleaned a huge amount from him: how valuable it can be when a pastor with more experience helps a younger one like this. Sometimes there were controversies to discuss and we didn't always agree. But it never affected the relationship. Often we would swap notes on people moving from one church to another – a helpful and important practice for neighbouring churches.

Mark could be wary of joint events and I think he was particularly averse to creating institutions which could get tired and formulaic. But increasingly he seemed to see the special opportunities which coalitions of evangelical churches could exploit for the gospel. I remember him being particularly insistent on going outside a limited conservative evangelical constituency to make such co-operation as broad as the gospel would allow.

He was not showy about it but there is one other aspect of his pastoral neighbourliness I must mention and perhaps it shows his greatness more than any other. Mark prayed for me and for Eden, virtually every day.

I can't ape Mark Ashton but I do hope one way or another I can be the sort of encourager to other pastors in town that he was to me.

Julian Hardyman is Senior Pastor of Eden Baptist Church, Cambridge.

*****

Equipping individuals for ministry

I was a parish assistant at StAG the year it became StAG (1993 to 1994). I well remember the move from the Round Church. I also remember Mark Ashton's lack of sentimentality for either building

– the only thing that mattered was that wherever we were would serve the gospel. I was very privileged during my short time on the staff to witness how this passion seemed to drive everything he did, and everything he asked us to do, down to the most apparently insignificant things. His attention to detail in so many areas – such as proof-reading the service sheets, the arrangement of the seating, his detailed instructions for the overhead projector operators – seemed excessive to me at first. Yet Mark's desire was that nothing should distract, nothing should make people feel ill at ease and that everything, down to the finest detail, should be outsider-friendly. The only offence to those coming through our doors was to be the 'offence' of the gospel (and in this he did not compromise!).

Coming from the more laid-back approach of college Christian Union, the almost military attention to detail and expectation of high standards in everything seemed at first a little harsh, inflexible, even 'unspiritual' to me. Yet I came to see that the extraordinary thought that had gone into the details stemmed from Mark's wholehearted passion for the gospel and for people to hear it (I suspect my preferred 'go-with-the-flow' approach stemmed more from laziness than spirituality). Realising that detailed gospel strategy can be borne out of deep gospel passion was an eye-opener for me.

I did, however, find the standards of excellence hard to cope with when, half way through the year, I became ill with a virus that gave me rather debilitating arthritic symptoms. I struggled with feeling my weakness in what suddenly felt like a very 'strong' church. In hindsight, I think the Lord let me experience this weakness for the sake of showing me my own pride but, at the time, StAG seemed to me to be a hard place to be weak. I do look back and realise the problem was largely my own – no-one ever made me *feel* weak, it was that I expected myself to be as strong as I (wrongly) perceived everyone else to be. The irony is that although Mark Ashton ran a pretty tight ship and strove for excellence in everything, he himself was the first to acknowledge his own weakness and sin. He was, in fact, one of the most real and honest people I have ever met. And when I wasn't able to do my job as I would have liked, he was only ever gentle and kind towards me. I have learnt much from Mark's preaching and example over the years but his persistent refusal to let anyone believe he was anything other than a weak and wretched sinner with a wonderful Saviour is probably the thing that I am most grateful for. Ultimately Mark Ashton has pointed me to a deeper grasp of the grace of God – the grace which frees us to be real before God about our sin, and then which spurs us on to live wholeheartedly for Him.

I found my time working with Mark and the staff team very helpful in equipping me for future ministry – initially with students and children at church alongside my job as a teacher; and later, in a full-time role as female student worker for seven years at St Ebbe's, Oxford. Invaluable lessons about Christian ministry were learnt during my parish assistant year: the conviction that the very best way to help others is to teach them to read the Bible and hear God speak into their lives; and the commitment to individuals in spending time building relationships and sharing our lives as Jesus did. Now, as a full-time wife and mum, these lessons continue to help and challenge me in seeking to serve Christ at home, in our church family and our community.

Sarah Collins (née Young) was a member of the Round/StAG (1989–99) as an undergraduate, on the staff as parish assistant and while working as a teacher. She is now a wife and mum, and a member of St Ebbe's in Headington, Oxford.

*****

Supporting and encouraging theological college students training for ministry

Those who were attached as theological college students to St Andrew the Great under Mark Ashton benefited from his special attention. Mark was careful to explain carefully to us the biblical foundation for all that shaped the ministry of the church, and he and Fiona provided for us a magnificent and unforgettable example of what it looked like to be a gospel minister actively leading a local church.

Among other key priorities, we learned first-hand from Mark and Fiona the power, centrality and sufficiency of God's word to accomplish God's work; the importance of prayer and humble dependence on the living God to provide for God's work; and the priority of a godly character and family life shaped according to God's word.

Mark Ashton's deep conviction in the power and sufficiency of God's word translated into practical hard work both in his own preaching and in the shaping of preachers for the future. Everybody knew that Friday was sacrosanct for Mark as he completed his own final preparation to preach on Sunday. The refusal to allow any disturbance provided a great model for those who were later to enter busy parish ministry. The same rigorous discipline applied by Mark to his own preaching was expected from us all. The script of each one of the sermons I preached as a placement student at StAG was carefully worked through with Mark in the week before it was delivered. Following the talk there would be carefully considered feedback with a few words of encouragement and areas for improvement. We all benefited substantially from his preaching classes held at the vicarage.

Mark Ashton's conviction that God's work should be self-evidently accomplished through God's power and in God's time rather than by human methods translated into both a discipline of prayerful dependence and deliberate decisions to keep the church family transparently dependent on God. There was never a sense of complacency – always a sense of seeking God's leading for the advance of the ministry. Human weakness as the necessary condition for the experience of divine power was a lesson learned by all who came close to the leadership of StAG.

Over the years Mark and Fiona shared their lives with literally hundreds of us, and the open home of the vicarage enables us to say that we 'followed his teaching, his conduct, his aim in life, his faith, his patience, his love, his steadfastness, and his persecutions.' He insisted that the integrity of the preacher's life and conduct was essential to the effectiveness of the preacher's ministry. A precious hour with Mark Ashton prior to our wedding taught Janet and me invaluable lessons that we have passed on to dozens of married couples. Of personal value was his apparently throwaway comment, 'William, God wants you to be a useful preacher when you are in your sixties. For that to happen, you will need to make a top priority of investing in your marriage throughout your ministry.'

This testimony of personal gratitude to God for the ministry of the Round Church and St Andrew the Great is one that could be repeated by countless individuals from around the world. Both Mark Ashton and Mark Ruston, together with numerous servants of the ministry in the church family, have enabled gospel fruit to be borne all over the world for many decades. May there be many more!

William Taylor was an undergraduate at the Round (1980–83), a theological student at Ridley Hall (1988–91) and is now Rector of St Helen's Bishopsgate, London.

*****

Supporting and encouraging visiting international scholars and students

StAG has served the wider church by striving to be an excellent, faithful local church. In Cambridge a large part of the church's context is determined by the presence of the university and the many international scholars and students. My strong memory is of Mark Ashton saying to me that the way that StAG could best minister to international students was by being the best local, family church it could. And so it worked to be.

StAG focused on building a church reflective of the gospel of the Lord Jesus Christ. The word of God was preached, people were served and encouraged to serve; exhortations to godly living and service of the Lord Jesus were given. It was welcoming, discerning, bold in proclamation and challenge and compassionate in conversation about the claims of Jesus on one's life. Pretty ordinary stuff in its own way but offered to all.

In addition to this, considerable time and energy spent working out how best to conduct a ministry to international students of all sorts: undergraduate, postgraduate and visiting scholars from every part of the globe. The congregation was accustomed to visitors and was hospitable, not least because of the example of the Ashtons. Most initiatives revolved around hospitality and Fiona Ashton's inexhaustible culinary skills, but also invariably included Bible teaching in both small and large groups. Through these groups and activities, some came to faith and many grew. For others perhaps it may have even helped them 'stay Christian', or at least grounded, amid some of the temptations that study at higher levels can sometimes bring.

I sense that the overall aim was to ensure that anyone who had contact with StAG was able to hear the gospel of the Lord Jesus

Christ and grow in their understanding and response to that gospel. While this would be of benefit to anyone who came within the orbit of StAG, the benefit for the wider church is clear – people would return from their involvement at StAG enhanced in their relationship with Jesus. They would do this having experienced a model of a church committed to helping outsiders come to know the living God and encouraging believers in seeking to live in obedience to Him. One of the incidental aspects of this which particularly struck me was StAG's insistence on keeping meetings as far as possible confined to one night only during the week so that there was plenty of time for congregation members to be involved with the 'world', their non-Christian neighbours and friends. Other more specific initiatives included an active Overseas Missions Group that met regularly to encourage prayer and supported many young people on short-term missions over the summer break, taking advantage of the proximity of the UK to much of the rest of the world.

Our family was grateful for this home away from home. We benefited from preaching that resisted the temptation to be 'clever' in the presence of so many students and scholars and instead spoke plainly and clearly the truths of the gospel to feed us. Amongst other opportunities to get involved we recall with gratitude the opportunities given to us to host a small group of new Christians in a discipleship course in our home. In the midst of a programme of study, this helped to keep our eyes on the 'main game', the purpose of the study in the context of Christian ministry.

I guess, in summary, StAG has benefited the wider church through its generous sharing of resources and its willing acceptance of the fact that for many the stay would be a relatively short-term one; and not only *not* resenting that reality, but actively embracing the opportunities to sustain and strengthen Christian faith and say farewell to those who sojourned briefly in their midst so that they might return home encouraged and, hopefully, a little (or a lot!) more mature and ministry-minded than when they arrived.

Bill Salier was a PhD student at StAG (1999–2001). He is now Vice-Principal of Moore College, Sydney, Australia and a member of St Barnabas, Broadway, Sydney.

CHAPTER 12

The next chapter

We end this account of what God has done through one particular church fellowship in Cambridge, England, over more than half a century with some extracts from the service of 'Institution and Induction' – the service in which Alasdair Paine was formally appointed and welcomed as the new minister at St Andrew the Great, held on 22 January 2011. Here are some words of thanks from Alasdair at that service:

> I have a personal great debt of gratitude under God to the ministry of this church. I want to express thanks to Jonathan Pryke who, when I was an undergraduate here in my first term at Cambridge in rooms in Trinity College in the parish of the Round Church, explained to me the glorious news of the gospel of the Lord Jesus. He was patient and careful and put up with my many questions and explained to me how I could come to have my sins forgiven and know God for myself. I thank you for that. Shortly after that, I was ushered round to 37 Jesus Lane where Mark Ruston welcomed me for tea and I quickly joined this church.

And one of his prayers from that service:

> *Our gracious God, we thank you for the ministry of the gospel of grace established in this congregation over so many years. We thank you for those who have gone before and who laboured in love for Jesus to make the glorious news of the gospel widely known. We thank you that from this place hundreds and hundreds have been sent out to serve you in this country and overseas. It is our prayer today that you, the Lord who is unchanging, will see to it that this same ministry continues. We pray for unity, for joy, for faithfulness and for effectiveness. In Jesus' name, Amen.*

And Alasdair's closing words:

> *I believe it's customary on these occasions to announce when church is happening tomorrow. 10 o'clock, 11.30 a.m. and 5 o'clock. And the word of God will be preached.*

To God be the glory!

APPENDIX – PERSONAL REFLECTIONS

Both Mark Ruston and Mark Ashton were held in deep affection by those who knew them. The following personal reflections are included in the hope that they will be food for thought, fuel for prayer – or simply encouragement to live the Christian life. Most importantly, it is hoped that they testify not to people's achievements but to the goodness of the God who loves us and sent his one and only Son to die for us that we might have eternal life.

The contributions come from a variety of sources – some have been written especially for this book, others are excerpts from letters written to Mark Ashton on hearing of his diagnosis of cancer (reproduced with permission). Some tell of conversion to Christ through the ministry of the Round/St Andrew the Great, others speak of the impact that God's word or godly living has had on their lives. Most are serious – some rather light-hearted! They span the decades and express gratitude to God for the ministries of both Marks.

We are grateful to all who have contributed. There are many others who could have told their own story of how they were blessed by being part of the church family at the Round/StAG – along with tales of all the mistakes made along the way. Of the adding of more contributors there could have been no end. We hope this is a sufficiently varied and encouraging selection of people and dates over the past half-century.

Personal reflections on the two Marks

Jonathan Fletcher

What an enormous privilege it was to have known both Mark Ruston and Mark Ashton very well indeed, albeit at different stages in their lives – and mine! Mark Ruston was my room leader on a Christian summer venture when I was a precocious fifteen-year-old. When I became a leader myself three years later, Mark was the first to begin training me. Eleven years after that, he invited me to be his curate and I had four wonderful years at the Round, receiving further training.

Mark Ruston, Vicar of the Round Church between 1955 and 1987.

I first met Mark Ashton when I was at Wycliffe Hall, Oxford; he had just arrived at Christ Church as an undergraduate to read English. Such was his confidence and presence that I assumed on our first encounter that he was teaching at the university! Christian friends pestered him so much to go along to Christian Union meetings that he was convinced they cared for him. Mark did not like or agree with what he heard but after a simple explanation of the gospel, on 7 February 1968, Mark slipped into Wycliffe Hall Chapel and, by himself, admitted his need of forgiveness, believed that Jesus had died on the cross in his place to make forgiveness possible, and simply came to Jesus, asking him to be his Lord and Saviour. I began reading the Bible with Mark week by week for the rest of my time at Oxford, and subsequently, I believe, we prayed for each other daily. Very graciously, Mark invited me back pretty regularly to preach at the Round/St Andrew the Great, and it was wonderful to see how his ministry flourished.

The two Marks were very different. Mark Ruston was a cheerful pessimist, usually expecting the worst but never getting down about it. Mark Ashton was a positive realist – very realistic about the daunting size of the work ahead, but positive about the possibility of achieving it. They had very different tasks. Mark Ruston began his ministry at the Round virtually from scratch. The Round had had no recent history as a flourishing evangelical student church, but that is what it became – bursting at the doors and needing a television overflow in the church hall across the road. Mark Ashton had the equally difficult task of succeeding a great pioneer and then building on and developing that ministry. Despite these differences, there were some great similarities:

Faithfulness to the gospel

At the end of their lives, both Marks were preaching the old, old gospel through which they themselves had been converted. Surely like so many others, they never 'moved on' – that is, they never moved away. It was the simple gospel of Jesus' death on the cross satisfying God's holy justice so that we might become children of God and then know and love the Lord Jesus. They both sat under Scripture and faithfully taught its truths. It could be said of them, as it was said of John the Baptist – 'they did no miracles but everything they said about Jesus was true' (cf John 10:41). Owing this mainly to their shared background at the Christian ventures run from Iwerne Minster, they held together the importance on the one hand of submitting to Scripture and teaching it accurately and, at the same time, having the right pietism that sought to feed on Christ in his blood and so come to love him and know him better.

Humility

Both Marks had grounds for pride. Their ministries were greatly used. They could have been puffed up. Both, however, were willing to undertake lowly, foot-washing ministry. During one Christian summer venture at Iwerne Minster, after a freak sand-storm had deposited its load from the Sahara on all the leaders' cars, a very senior Mark Ruston was seen at 7.30 a.m. going from car to car, washing all the windscreens. Mark Ashton similarly continued to serve on Christian ventures, as did Mark Ruston, right up to the summer before he died. Neither sought preferment as they were destitute of that awful ecclesiastical blight of ungodly ambition or recognition on a larger, national platform. Mark Ruston did indeed become a Canon and an honorary chaplain to the Queen but made little of it. Mark Ashton steadfastly refused the offer of a canonry, to the great astonishment of his bishop. When hearing of a brother's serious moral lapse, Mark Ruston said to me, 'There, but for the grace of God, go I.' Mark Ashton, who had become aware of his battle with pride during his gap year in Pakistan, fought that particular temptation victoriously.

In different ways, their humility shone forth as servants of the Cambridge Inter-Collegiate Christian Union (CICCU). The professional would always be able to do it better than the amateur but instead of taking over the student work, they acted as supporting servants. Mark Ruston supported the

Mark Ashton, Vicar of the Round Church and St Andrew the Great between 1987 and 2010.

CICCU not just in word but by his physical presence every Saturday evening at the CICCU 'Bible Reading' in the Union Society Debating Chamber. Similarly, Mark Ashton while at Ridley Hall, in no way played the role of 'elder statesman' of the CICCU but, by attendance every Saturday and Sunday evening and by welcoming at the door, was their servant.

Love

Everybody who knew both Marks would want to testify to the generosity of their friendship and practical kindness. When this curate got back late at night from his holiday, Mark Ruston had made sure he would find a bottle of fresh milk in his fridge. Mark Ruston was a past-master at personal work and along with Mark Ashton was incredibly shrewd in perceptive assessment and wise counsel. 'Faithful are the wounds of a friend' (Prov. 27:6). Both Marks showed this loving friendship by being willing to evaluate and pass on positive criticisms and suggestions. At the end of my first Christian camp as a leader under his supervision, I received from Mark Ruston two sides of A4 with 'crits and suggs' – mainly 'crits' – on how I had performed. At the end of my first year as his curate, I received four sides of A4 with similar criticisms and suggestions. They were faithful wounds – but wonderfully carried no offence. One of the unnerving consequences of being an occasional visiting preacher for Mark Ashton was the letter that arrived shortly afterwards, though this Mark's critical concerns tended to be concentrated more on the length of the sermon than on its contents! This faithful love meant that I could count totally on their loyalty. They would have defended me to the last ditch.

Courage

'He who stands closest to his captain is a sure target for the archers.' It takes courage to stand up for conservative evangelicalism. I witnessed Mark Ruston at a meeting of Deans and Chaplains, many of whom were hostile to the CICCU. Almost single-handedly, Mark went in to bat for these slightly over-enthusiastic but nevertheless totally gospel-hearted undergraduates. Similarly, as a founding member of the Council of Reform, that crusading movement seeking to restore the Church of England to its evangelical roots, Mark Ashton did not hesitate, albeit always graciously, to contend for the faith once for all delivered to the saints. I would have loved to have been there as a fly on the wall as with different bishops Mark stood his ground and fought for himself and even more for others.

For many of us, the greatest challenge of the courage of both Marks was the way they faced up to their deaths. In one sense it was not courage, it was their quiet assurance of going home to be with Christ. Although that prospect filled their horizon, they were both aware that the last part of the journey would be difficult, but, in increasing weakness and dependence, their courage and their confidence shone through triumphantly.

What a wonderful heritage they have both left behind. What a blessing to have known them.

Jonathan Fletcher was a curate at the Round (1972–76) and incumbent of Emmanuel, Wimbledon (1982–2012).

Reflections on 1955 to 1987
and Mark Ruston

*H*onour is an old-fashioned word but it comes to mind when thinking of Mark Ruston. I honour him for his gift of friendship, his pastoral heart and the simplicity and directness of his personal walk with Christ. He was an ideal holiday companion and his humour was never very far away.

I honour Mark Ruston too for the example he set, often quite unknowingly, of cheerfulness, of making the best of things and thinking the best of people, and of doing a job properly. George Herbert's hymn makes me think of him:

> *A servant with this clause*
> *makes drudgery divine;*
> *who sweeps a room, as for thy laws,*
> *makes that and the action fine.*

Mark was always ready to serve: if a boy was sick on the floor at any Christian summer venture or house party where Mark was among the leaders, as often as not, it would be he who unobtrusively set to and cleaned it up.

I honour him too for his self-effacing humility and single-mindedness in the cause of Christ. You can see in 'Crockford's'[1] that, having spent ten years as a school chaplain and been chaplain to two Cambridge colleges, he reverted in 1954 to the role of assistant curate, putting the clock back a dozen years to resume the most junior post in the ordained ministry. He did this, so I believe, because he felt sure God still had work for him to do in Cambridge; and that he should wait there, submissively, until his future was made plain. A year later, he was appointed Vicar of the Round.

From that moment, I think, Mark Ruston was in no doubt that this was where God had called him. Ten years later, I tried to persuade him to allow his name to be considered as successor to the hugely influential Canon T.G. Mohan, long-serving Secretary of the Church Pastoral-Aid Society (I was at that time on its staff). But no, he had no calling to leave the growing work at the Round, for which he was so exactly a round peg in a very circular hole. Seven or eight years after that, approached (as I understand) about a bishopric, his answer was the same. Only the requests to become Rural Dean of Cambridge, or Examining Chaplain, or Honorary Canon of Ely Cathedral, or a Chaplain to Her Majesty the Queen were accepted, because they did not take him from his ministry to 'town and gown', the pastoring, preaching and teaching in Cambridge which he knew to be his calling.

I used to visit him from Norfolk a number of times each year, and latterly we often talked about his retirement. I think it is no secret that he was uncharacteristically hesitant and indecisive, reluctant to make up his mind. This was because, so I learned, he knew the man he wanted to take over his work, and was determined to hold on until this seemed assured. So, in 1987, Mark succeeded Mark. How right Mark Ruston had been!

Timothy Dudley-Smith, lifelong friend of Mark Ruston, hymn writer, former Bishop of Thetford and member of St Michael's, Winterbourne Earls, Salisbury.

*****

Appendix – personal reflections

An extract from the address at Mark Ruston's funeral and thanksgiving service

Today we lay to rest all that is mortal of Mark, born in World War 1 on 23 August 1916, until his Lord called him home at seventy-three years old, on 3 January 1990. All that is immortal of Mark

is now rejoicing in the immediate presence of the Master he served so faithfully since his clear-cut conversion at sixteen at one of Mr Nash's earliest camps in the 1930s.[2]

For his funeral, Mark chose 2 Corinthians 4 and 5 himself and, with the directness and the honesty that was such a daunting and also a delightful part of Mark's character, he would want us to be in no doubt about his own testimony: 'We know that if the earthly tent we live in is destroyed' (and he faced that destruction by cancer of his earthly tabernacle or tent with all the steadfast courage with which he faced all difficul-

Mark Ruston at the Round Church in 1981, where he was Vicar for thirty-two years.

ties). Then, 'we have a (permanent) building from God', a house not made with hands, eternal in the heavens... 'so what is mortal may be swallowed up by life' (2 Cor. 5:1–4). Life eternal, the very life abundant which Mark experienced when, as a senior school boy, he first welcomed the Lord Jesus into his heart as Saviour and Lord and began serving him right on from that day until his home call into the fullness of service, which is night and day in his presence. And ever since, his chief joy and over-riding purpose – without prejudice, without embarrassing piety, without unnecessary emotional pressure – has been to preach Christ and him crucified, and to call to Jesus young and old, students and school-boys, at Cheltenham College, Jesus College, Wengen, East Africa, at Islington, at Iwerne Minster and supremely for over thirty years here at the Round Church in Cambridge. He called people to Jesus and he was never tired of explaining Revelation 3:20, 'Behold! I stand at the door and knock. If any man hear my voice and open the door, I will come in to him and sup with him, and he with me.'

...Personal evangelism was his high aim, his serious purpose and his abiding joy. This kept him spiritually fresh right through to the end of his earthly journey towards heaven. And in this great crowd... there must be scores of men and women too who would want to say today, 'Mark led me to Christ'. Or 'Mark brought me to assurance of salvation'. Or 'Mark encouraged me to offer for Christian service'. Or 'Mark challenged me to consider ordination.'

...Mark gave himself first to camp work (and, our gain, these last few years even more camp work after retirement) and then to student work and work among young families, refusing the invitation to 'high office' in the church as it's sometimes called. Though he was, of course, made a Queen's Honorary Chaplain, as you know. And yet I would judge that Mark is the Charles Simeon of our generation in Cambridge. And it was said of Charles Simeon that 'his influence is greater than any primate', as Macaulay the historian put it. And I would judge this to be true for Mark.

...It is interesting that Mark, for his entire steadfast steadiness, was in fact an innovator in the church (his student assistants, now copied elsewhere, are an example). And thirty or forty years before the stress on inner city work, Mark from the Round and Basil Gough at St Ebbe's, Oxford, collected Oxbridge students to come and spend a week with us in the Islington Deanery (long before its gentrification!).

...In his no-nonsense, humble way, Mark asked if I would say 'sorry' to anyone whom he had been hard on, in advice or criticism which, he said, had not been wholly justified. Yet we who are his friends, young or contemporary, would rather have received firm advice from Mark, than to have had no-one caring pastorally for our souls. Because we all knew that bravely he was challenging himself first and us second, to practical, scriptural, Christ-centred holiness. He lived as he taught, so we honoured and respected as well as loved him.

Maurice Wood (1916–2007), lifelong friend of Mark Ruston, former principal of Oak Hill Theological College and Bishop of Norwich.

Appendix – personal reflections

Soon after arriving in Cambridge, I was visited by a couple of men from the Christian Union and from them I first heard the gospel in terms I could begin to understand. They helped me get settled in at the university and also they took a spiritual interest in me. Robert Footner took me to the Round Church one Sunday. It was 25 October 1955 and Mark Ruston preached. Robert and I wandered back to St Catherine's with about twenty minutes to spare before college breakfast and went up to Robbie's bedsitter to 'kill the time', as it were. Well, we killed it alright! Robert challenged me first with whether I knew Christ personally, which mystified me, and I had to indicate that I didn't. Then he challenged me as to whether I had ever 'surrendered' my life to Christ. I am sure the service at the Round and Mark Ruston's preaching set me up for what happened in those next minutes. I knelt in Robbie's bedsitter and invited Jesus Christ into my life as my Lord and Saviour. This was a Damascus Road moment and life-changing experience for me. Thereafter the Round became my parish church during my undergraduate years. I remember going round to Mark Ruston's warm and cosy house for tea and crumpets on a black and wintry Cambridge afternoon. I was perplexed about my calling and future and how to discern it. I was thinking about being a schoolmaster. Mark encouraged me not to be impetuous as to what the Lord's final call to me would be. He was gracious, gentle and pastoral. We ended with a lovely time of prayer. It was an important conversation for me. In the event, the Lord has led me over these last fifty years into a very clear call to evangelism in the cities of Africa, through African Enterprise, an organisation I founded. I have little doubt that I am just one of hundreds if not thousands of students that Mark Ruston and the Round touched in similar ways. So I honour him, the church and the legacy which has come down out of all those years when he was Rector. What a man and what a ministry to remember! Deo gloria! Deo gratias!

Michael Cassidy, undergraduate at Cambridge (1955–58), Founder and former International Team Leader of Africa Enterprise, member of Church of the Ascension, Anglican Diocese of Natal, Hilton, South Africa.

I first met Mark Ruston when he came to speak at the Stowe School Christian meeting. I was immediately attracted to his Christlikeness and warmth of character. As a rather precocious fourteen-year-old, I talked to him about 'joining the ministry'. He wrote to me soon after and gently encouraged me to concentrate on service at school: 'Ministry is only the same thing as service – the Greek word means both. Loyalty to the (Christian) meeting is service. So is bringing friends along to it. And prayer; and of course (the hardest bit!), living a Christian life is the best service of all – 'letting your light shine, so that...? What? See Matthew 5:14–16.'

I wrote to him concerned about whether I had received the Holy Spirit, having read Chuck Colson's book *Born Again*. His reply shows his remarkable ability to make theology simple and accessible to a teenager: 'Meanwhile, on your question about Colson and the Holy Spirit: I have got good news – you have Him (not 'it')! You cannot carve up the Trinity; and Father, Son and Holy Spirit are one God. If you "accept Jesus", He comes to you not in the physical form of Jesus but as the Holy Spirit (Romans 8:9 puts it negatively)... The question is not, "Have I got Him?" but "Has He got all of me?" Someone described the Spirit as Jesus' "other self" – and that's just about it!' I was also concerned about a friend who had dropped me because I was pushing a bit too hard to win him for Christ. Mark's pastoral wisdom shines through: 'I can only say keep friendly and unpressing over your friend. Sadly it takes two to make a friendship.'

I eventually ended up at Ridley Hall in Cambridge just after Mark Ruston had retired. I saw a lot of him one way and another. He was a wonderful friend and *confidant*. I especially remember going to see him after some disappointment. I self-pityingly poured out my woes and grievances and Mark hardly said a word. After a long and rather awkward silence, he simply said, 'Oh dear, it's all very difficult, isn't it?' And that was an end to the matter which helped me to move on and stop feeling sorry for myself. Most of all, I know he prayed for me. I can only begin to imagine what I owe to those prayers.

Richard Coombs, theological student at Ridley Hall (1987–90), now Vicar of St John the Baptist, Burford.

Appendix – personal reflections

As a new convert, I was taken to the Round Church by the friend who led me to Christ. A couple of weeks later Mark Ruston greeted me at the door after a service with his Filofax diary open and I was 'booked in' for a cup of tea. I had never been to tea with a vicar before and didn't know what to expect. Mark had a wonderful knack though of putting people at their ease without dodging the issue. I left some forty-five minutes later encouraged, reassured and persuaded against all my better judgement that I should be letting my friends know about this Christ I had come to trust and hardly knew myself. It was my first experience of the gospel steel and sharpness that lay underneath his warm, gentle smile.

Mark Ruston was everything that 'flash' is not! His was a model of faithful ministry; gracious, steady wisdom, constant, quiet encouragement, long-term disciplined praying and persevering gospel teaching and personal work.

Hugh Palmer, undergraduate at the Round (1970–72), Rector, All Souls Langham Place, London.

*****

The Round Church played a significant role in my new Christian life after I came to faith in my first year at Cambridge. Jonathan Fletcher was the curate at the time and, after my encounter with Jesus through reading the New Testament, Jonathan met with me once a week for a year, then fortnightly in the second year and every month in the third year. He answered my questions patiently, lent me books and encouraged me in my faith. Mark Ruston was the gracious and godly vicar at the time.

Nicky Gumbel, undergraduate at the Round (1973–76), now Vicar, Holy Trinity Brompton, London.

*****

I would like to mention two aspects of the ministry of the Round – first, the church's support of young people, and second, the way the Round was a 'sending' church. I became a Christian through the witness of a friend at the Perse School, Cambridge.

I came along to the Round and after evening services would go along to SCA (the *Schoolmembers' Christian Association*), founded by David Watson, which met alternately in the Round Church Hall and in various homes as a kind of house group. The encouragement and support of the Round and SCA nurtured many of my contemporaries in the early years of faith at school and university. Most of us are still Christians and have leadership roles of some sort in our churches. Second, many people will remember the curates and pastoral workers who worked so diligently and went on to serve God in other roles, and will be thanking God for the Round as a 'sending' church.

Shaun De Boo, member of the Round (1976–84), now member of Brentwood Baptist Church, Chartered Accountant.

*****

I had the enormous privilege of working as Graduate Assistant at the Round Church in Cambridge for two years in the 1980s. My father had been converted through the Cambridge Inter-Collegiate Christian Union (CICCU) at the beginning of his first year; and the chaplain of his college, Jesus College, had been Mark Ruston. My father recalls that prioritising personal work was a hallmark of Mark's ministry: he is sure that Mark, through the CICCU, arranged for an older student to study the Bible with him one-to-one and then Mark invited my father to go to a Christian summer venture run by Mr Nash. They remained friends until Mark's death.

Thirty years after my father's conversion Mark Ruston wrote to me (letter writing was another key ingredient of his ministry) inviting me to 'leave the fleshpots of London' (his words) to work at the Round. As a young graduate, I was slightly shy of this retiring, disciplined godly man, but was soon to discover he had a great sense of humour and endearing eccentricities (part of the job was doing Mark's shopping and only Cathedral City Cheddar would do!)

But, above all, it was by his example and teaching I learnt so much. He had a passion that people come to have a personal trust in the Lord Jesus Christ, to be built up in him and then to go out and serve, and to have a deep love of the Bible as the place where we come to hear the Lord Jesus speaking to us. He was strategic – urging me to invite girls to Christian holiday ventures. He knew that there they would hear the gospel, learn and be trained to serve. He would encourage me to contact a particular individual and study the Bible one-to-one with them, but above all his love and care and prayer for individuals and his persevering with them was an example that struck home.

Sarah Farrar-Bell (née Wilson), graduate assistant at the Round (1983– 85), wife to Charlie and mother to three nearly grown up children and part-time women's worker at Christ Church, Mayfair.

*****

When Mark Ruston retired as Vicar of the Round Church, he spent several months travelling the world. On his return he informed me, in his usual self-effacing and understated way, that he had spent only two nights in places other than the homes of Christian men whose lives had been impacted through the ministry of the Round Church. Such has been the 'reach' of the Round Church and St Andrew the Great. It has often been noted that Mark Ruston's most powerfully used gift was his faithful and consistent commitment to the discipleship of the individual. There can be few clearer examples of what it means to 'bear fruit with patience'.

As a personal beneficiary, I have vivid memories of the impact of a card with a line of simple encouragement, a timely rebuke or encouragement; noticing a slightly over-sized diary he would gently suggest 'you must be important, my dear'; and the willingness to listen week after week to the immature burbling of a young one-to-one Bible student while regularly prompting with 'and have you noticed, my dear, verse five?' This would be followed by three carefully prepared points, each one perfectly tailored to instruct and encourage. I once heard him giving a talk on the subject of personal work and one of his most memorable pieces of advice was 'pray before, pray during, pray afterwards'.

His remark at a school mission in 1986 gives particular insight into his ministry strategy. Speaking of a fifth former he said: 'Each one is a multiplication table'. He meant that time invested in the fifteen-year-old individual might, under God, reap a harvest thirty, sixty or a hundredfold.

This radical focus on the individual in the ministry of the Round Church and St Andrew the Great has seen good soil producing bumper harvests in countless nations over many decades.

William Taylor, undergraduate at the Round (1980–83), theological student at Ridley Hall (1988–91), Rector, St Helen's Bishopsgate, London.

*****

The Reverend Cuthbert Mark Ruston – known in the family as 'Uncle Mark' – became my godfather in 1961. He never married, but he acquired a number of godchildren. At my Anglican service of baptism, along with my parents and my aunts, he promised to declare his faith in God the Father, Son and Holy Spirit; and to renounce 'the devil and all his works'. He affirmed his belief in the crucifixion, resurrection, ascension and second coming of Christ. My godfather promised, on my behalf, to serve God according to his 'holy will'. As in all matters of faith, it was not something he undertook lightly.

Years later, Uncle Mark would speak to me of his godchildren, explaining how he prayed for us all. As we grew older and came to be confirmed, he delighted in the fact that his prayers had been answered and that we were ready to stand up for Jesus, as believing individuals in our own right. My godfather may have relinquished his formal duties at that point, but he never tired of praying for us and offering Christian friendship and wise counsel.

On one occasion, my husband David and I were 'between homes' and we were invited to my godfather's house for a few days, while he was away. A homeless man appeared on the doorstep one night, adamant that there was some special treatment that he was usually offered. Not wanting to rock any boats, we rang the curate, who came round instantly and took charge. It was clear that my godfather delighted in giving a welcome to all-comers.

Caroline Gill (née Dudley-Smith), god-daughter of Mark Ruston, member of the Round (1990–92), member of the Waterfront Benefice in Ipswich, where her archaeologist husband, David, is a Reader.

Appendix – personal reflections

Despite being an undergraduate and postgraduate student at Cambridge, my memories of the Round are of a church for families as well as students. My path to faith was via Crusaders, the Discoverer's Cruise (a Christian holiday on the Norfolk Broads at Easter-time) and Billy Graham in 1967. The Round became my home church, especially the evening service, which was followed by SCA (*Schoolmembers' Christian Association*) which met in the church hall and drew together fifth and sixth formers from across the city, belonging to a range of churches, or none. Crusaders, SCA and the Round all gave me fundamental biblical truth in a thorough, but accessible and relevant way. A key constant through my time at the Round was the loving and persistent ministry of Mark Ruston backed by curates such as David Huggett and Jonathan Fletcher. Mark Ruston exercised a gentle but attentive pastoral care of the home congregation as much as the term-time students. At Christmas he would give a book, carefully chosen to encourage our discipleship. There was a full range of teaching with no hard topic ducked, but almost always coming back to the demands of the gospel in a natural way. I am sure I am just one of many who owe a huge debt to Mark Ruston's sacrificial pursuit of his ministry.

John Glauert, member of the Round as schoolboy (1971-73), undergraduate (1973-76) and postgraduate (1978-81). Now Professor of Computing Sciences at University of East Anglia, and attending Holy Trinity, Norwich.

*****

Memories of Mark Ruston: listening with keen interest and kindly patience as an eighteen-year-old shyly managed to explain that he'd asked Jesus to be his Lord. Running a short course for new believers – full of Scripture and fresh, sane faith. Reading the lesson at the Round Church – one of the things he said he enjoyed most. Taking on a fresh lease of life on a ski party and giving thirteen-year-olds a memorable talk on 'How to ski uphill'. Preaching – careful, prayerful, painstakingly prepared. Long hours of preparation – often including a very long Saturday, glimpsed as a lodger at 37 Jesus Lane. A gracious, patient landlord – even when in his absence I unfortunately told the coal man to empty his sacks into Mark's bike shed! Working his way through the post with a periodic 'humph!' while his toast cooled down outside on the window-sill – not a morning conversationalist. The ringing of the phone at about nine o'clock, another 'humph!' and off to work.

John Hutchison, undergraduate at the Round (1971–75), and Mark Ruston's lodger (1974–75), Chaplain, Sheffield Children's Hospital.

*****

We are often reminded that the church is not the building, it's the people, the living stones (1 Pet. 2:5). It has been people whose

strengths God has used to shape the ministry of the Round Church and then St Andrew the Great. We mention a few here:

A former churchwarden, Doc Adamson, used to place low-value coins in the collection plate so that the young people could do the same without embarrassment. Many of those young people went on to church leadership, both lay and ordained. The Family Services in the 1970s and early 1980s were all All-Age Services until curate Nigel Holmes encouraged the setting up of separate teaching groups for the children. These groups set a pattern

Mark Ruston (1916-1990), at a Christian summer venture at Iwerne Minster in 1986.

for subsequent youth and children's work – not only at StAG but also at its church plants in and around Cambridge. *Travs*, for example, provided positive, inspirational Christian role models for the teenagers.

Other curates too left their mark. The hospitality offered by the Huggetts and the Lennons to *Focus* – a group for the under-thirties – was a lesson learned by many who now willingly use their home for God. What of the parish assistants? What an impact there has been since Sandy Nichol (now Hames) was appointed by Mark Ruston as a part-time parish assistant to support the ministry to female students. Many former parish assistants are now in ordained ministry. This effective way of preparing young men and women to serve the church has developed from that small beginning to more formal structures such as the 9:38 web.[3]

Mark Ruston suggested that a summer coffee bar be held in the Round Church Hall for language school students. This was the start of one of the streams that eventually flowed into what has become the wide-ranging work with international students in Cambridge. This work now operates throughout the year under the Friends International banner.

Although student work remains the most significant aspect of the ministry at StAG, outreach to others in the Cambridge community became an important feature. For example, Bounce-A-Round for mums and toddlers was spearheaded by Fiona Ashton and has been used by God to draw many to faith.

In 1 Corinthians 3:6, Paul writes, 'I planted the seed, Apollos watered it, but God made it grow.' The same can be said of the Round Church and StAG. Mark Ruston planted many seeds which were enhanced and developed by Mark Ashton. And God has indeed been making them grow. We trust and pray that he will continue to do so in the years ahead.

John Stanton, member of the Round/StAG since 1972 and Polly Stanton, member since 1971, moved with other StAG members to All Saints, Little Shelford in 1997. John is Consultant Engineer and Polly is Administrator, Faraday Institute.

*****

I had a very brief but highly significant encounter with Mark Ruston. The summer before I came up to Cambridge, I visited the Round Church with my father, and Mark Ruston made the effort to come up, unannounced, greet me by name and say that he was looking forward to my coming up next term. I knew straightaway that someone was going to look after me. I think Mark Ruston's approach to me by name was indicative of his particular pastoral touch. I'm pretty sure that he had done research on the upcoming 'freshers' (first year students), knew my family, spotted my father, put two and two together and made an effort to make me feel at home. I gather that he used to keep a file card list of all newcomers he met on Sunday, annotated with physical descriptions, which he would pass around the staff table the following week to find out people's names. He was quite remarkable.

Josh Moody, in Cambridge as undergraduate (1987–92) and post-graduate (1994–97), now Senior Pastor of College Church, Wheaton, Illinois.

*****

We attended diligently but, in truth, our roots didn't go deep – not helped by Keith's job taking us overseas for lengthy periods – until we switched to the family service when our first daughter, Claire, was born. We enjoyed the family services. They were informal. They did seem to be a clergy-free zone, though; we probably sensed we were not quite as 'key' as the student service. We began to make good relationships with those around us and to learn of the servant role a Christian has. This was a great step towards becoming mature adult members of the Christian family.

Keith and Sarah Haddow, members of the Round/StAG (1982–97), moved with other members of StAG to All Saints, Little Shelford, in 1997. Keith is a financial director and Sarah is a school teacher.

*****

In the 1960s and 1970s the Round Church services were formal and traditional. Mark Ruston always encouraged lay participation but was insistent on a proper dress code. One conversation which I recall went like this: 'John, would you read the first lesson?' 'Yes, but it is a bit short notice.' (We were just about to process into church from the vestry.) 'Quite right, but I know I can rely on you. Wait a moment. Oh, I am sorry, but you really cannot read this morning – you aren't wearing a jacket or tie and I'm not sure that those denim jean trousers are appropriate. Could you come properly dressed this evening?' How times have changed!

John Anstead, member of the Round/StAG (1966–2008), moved with other StAG members to St Matthew's, Cambridge, retired teacher.

Appendix – personal reflections

*****

Mark Ruston was very fond of good cooking and often had special guests to meals. His problem was providing tasty food which was not shop bought. The solution came about in this way:

Mark: Sara, I want to ask you... um... I want to ask you... Don't you think that bought cakes are rather expensive and not very nice?
Sara: Yes.
Mark: Well, I thought I would make a list of all the ladies who could make me cakes. Then I crossed out all the ones who weren't married (they might get the wrong idea) and then I crossed out the ones who couldn't cook and that left you!
Sara: So you would like me to make you a cake sometimes?
Mark: Yes, but we need a plan. I know! If I wink at you during the Te Deum, then that would be a signal that I would like a cake!

And so it came to pass that Mark Ruston had homemade cakes for special teas.

Sara Anstead, member of the Round/StAG (1966–2008), moved with other StAG members to St Matthew's, Cambridge, retired teacher.

Endnotes

1. See note 1 on p. 51.

2. 'Camp' refers to the Christian summer ventures that Mark was involved with throughout his life, mostly held at Iwerne Minster in Dorset, which gave public school boys the opportunity to hear and respond to the claims of the Lord Jesus Christ.

3. 9:38 was set up in response to Jesus' command to 'ask the Lord of the Harvest to send out workers into His harvest field' because 'the harvest is plentiful but the workers are few' (Matt. 9:37-38). It runs conferences to help Christians consider full-time gospel ministry and help churches set up church-based ministry training schemes.

Reflections on 1987 to 2010
and Mark Ashton

'Lucy, don't delay any longer.' The words were spoken by Mark Ashton to a tearful twenty-year-old student in a small tower room at the top of the Union Society. I had been coming to the Round Church services there off and on for about six months, as well as various Cambridge Inter-Collegiate Christian Union evangelistic meetings. Despite my church-going upbringing, I had come to realise that my allegiance to Christianity was not the same as personal submission to Jesus as Lord and Saviour. I had been intrigued by the living faith I had encountered in student friends and accompanied them to church. Mark Ashton's clear explanation of the Bible week after week gradually swept away the objections and doubts that I raised, though inexplicably (to me at the time) brought tears almost every week. But still I delayed actually taking the plunge, putting my life into Jesus' hands. After one service Mark Ashton invited anyone interested in knowing more to come up to the tower room. With a nudge from a friend, I went up, attempting to hide my tears. Mark tactfully did not address me during the discussion but spoke to me gently and firmly as I left the room last. He had been watching, he knew me. He knew just what I needed. I went straight to my room and knelt and submitted my life to Christ.

Lucy Chapman (née Maunsell), undergraduate at the Round (1988–91). Lucy is raising three children and serving the church alongside her husband Tim at Christ Church, South Cambs, Sawston.

*****

Our son, a member of StAG, introduced us to the church when we were in our fifties. For different reasons, we both felt that something was missing from our lives. We had serious concerns about the formality and rigidity of 'church' but, to our surprise, we quickly felt comfortable in the services and subsequently in the church groups we joined. We found that the sermons were really saying something to us. Mark Ashton led the way in looking in depth at God's word, making it relevant to life today, emphasising what Jesus has done for us, how we can worship him and serve him in our daily lives. The leadership emphasised that every member has a valuable contribution to make, and this encouraged a feeling of 'belonging'. We came to understand that 'being a Christian' is not about keeping rules or restricting freedom. Jesus tells us, 'I am the way and the truth and the life' (John 14:16). He offers us the only pathway to God the Father. We learnt that because of Jesus' sacrifice at the cross, God forgives our sins and we can be part of his family. This brings ultimate freedom and great joy, as we have discovered. StAG's outward-looking approach encourages us to share this joy with others.

Charles and Pauline Burling, members of StAG since 2003, both now retired.

*****

It was at the Round Church that I heard the good news of Christ clearly explained by a passionate, loud and deadly sincere man. He seemed to know just what I was thinking and what my excuses for rejecting Christianity would be and he relentlessly addressed them. God was clearly at work bringing me to a conviction of sin. No doubt there were other factors involved but what I remember was, week in week out, earnest Bible teaching that held me sometimes amazed, often incensed (though I would never let that show), but always compelled me to come back to hear what God would say next.

Tim Chapman, undergraduate at the Round (1988–91), now Minister, Christ Church, South Cambs, Sawston.

*****

It is perhaps worth mentioning a couple of particular aspects of Mark Ashton's time in south London when he was General Secretary of CYFA (Christian Youth Fellowship Association) since

Mark and Fiona Ashton

this phase had a significant effect on Mark's later ministry. At CYFA, Mark was involved in their summer Christian holidays for children and young people, which were a wonderful training ground for his hand-picked team of leaders – both ordained and lay – and, of course, for the youngsters attending. At that time, he was also Honorary Curate at St Stephen's, Clapham Park. He had a major legacy in biblical preaching, a strong youth group with a majority of black youngsters and their steel band, and a home Bible study group beyond comparison. All this, on top of his 'day job'. I write as one greatly blessed by Mark and Fiona's presence in south London – and subsequently.

Guy Abel, friend of Mark and Fiona Ashton from St Stephen's, Clapham Park, retired from employment, member of Bethlehem Baptist Church, Tauranga, New Zealand.

*****

Several years ago, I spoke at a series of conventions in Singapore and at various churches. Those of you who have had this privilege know that the churches there are active and vibrant.

When I came away, I felt that I had been ministered to rather than the reverse. At every church I visited, there were keen elders in leadership roles. Nearly all of them were professional people. I asked them, one by one, how they had come to Christ. I discovered, to my surprise, that they were all converted when they were at university overseas. Most of them were at either at Oxford or Cambridge. Where did they go to church in Cambridge? StAG. It is hard for us to understand in the western churches how significant this is. Every overseas undergraduate will be a leader when they return home after graduation. This is true in many cases in our own country but it is more so in the developing countries. If ever I needed convincing of the importance of work with overseas students, this trip persuaded me. They are a wonderful mission field on our doorstep.

John Chapman, friend of Mark and Fiona Ashton and Australian evangelist, member of Engadine Anglican Church, Sydney. John spoke at a series of events during the week-long mission to mark the opening of the newly restored St Andrew the Great building in January 1994.

*****

Mark Ashton's conviction was that since God inspired whole Bible books with their own overall message, we should preach whole Bible books, passage by passage, so that our congregations take in their overall message. He believed topical teaching has a place, but insisted that only a diet of predominantly sequential preaching will protect a church from the subjective emphases and blind spots of its preachers. Only predominantly sequential preaching makes preachers teach the whole counsel of God – including things they might neither choose nor want to speak on. That's why neither Family Services nor Guest Services would (generally) interrupt a series in a Bible book, but be part of it – reflecting Mark Ashton's equal conviction that all ages could be addressed and evangelised from anywhere in the Bible.

Sequential preaching also protects against a guru mentality: Mark Ashton fostered the atmosphere that we were there not to hear what he thought, but what the Bible says. That freed the rest of us who preached from aiming to 'be Mark' – and, instead, to do what Mark modelled. And that's why I remember him saying, 'I don't want people coming because of who's down to preach on the term card. I want people coming for the Bible.'

Ian Garrett, on the staff as pastoral assistant at StAG (1992–94), now Assistant Minister, Jesmond Parish Church, Newcastle.

*****

When the Round Church congregation decided to move to St Andrew the Great, much prayer, time and effort were put into trying to ensure that the Round Church building continued to be used as an on-going, breathing witness for Christ and his gospel. Initially it was suggested that the building might be suitably altered to provide a Christian bookshop. Unfortunately, English Heritage was not happy about this (among other things, they considered the 'Salvin' restoration pews from 1843 to be indispensable) so the Christian bookshop idea had to be shelved.

In the ensuing uncertainty, an alternative was considered – to create a Christian heritage centre in the heart of the city. In January 2001, Christian Heritage was granted a licence and work began. Through displays and videos in the church building itself, guided walks through the city (pointing out the rich Christian history of the city and university – just consider, for example, the colleges with names like Jesus, Christ's, Trinity, Emmanuel), lectures and student internships, Christian Heritage aims to show that the gospel of Jesus Christ is still our best legacy from the past and the most reliable antidote to our current intellectual and moral infections.

Ranald Macaulay, Founder of Christian Heritage, Round Church, Cambridge.

*****

I joined StAG as Administrator three weeks after moving to Cambridge from the United States. It was the grace-filled attitude of the staff and congregation which made working at StAG notably different to previous jobs (mostly in Christian organisations). They were not afraid of confrontation when necessary but, after apologies were made, there was genuine forgiveness and a coming together to fix and learn from mistakes and move on. StAG's consistent emphasis on our dependence upon God's grace meant that there was room for openness and honesty. I found myself being met where I was and encouraged to grow and mature, both professionally and as a Christian. Mark Ashton used to tell the staff that when mentoring someone spiritually, we should never assume that they are reading their Bible or praying regularly or living lives of faithful obedience to Christ; we should instead begin by acknowledging together that it is difficult to do these things, to change and to discipline ourselves.

Administration can easily take over an organisation. At StAG I was encouraged to scrutinise my work and was given the freedom to decide whether something actually needed to be done. I was told to view my work through the lens of our mission statement: a commitment to the Bible and prayer; our mission to the academic communities; and to mature discipleship for all. Only some of my own work could be considered front-line gospel work; but Mark Ashton and others helped me see the significance of even mundane tasks by considering everything in terms of its potential to contribute to StAG's central mission. My administrative job, then, was primarily about freeing up congregation and staff to spread the gospel and care for others and, above all – as Mark Ashton often put it – 'to keep the preachers preaching'.

Stacey Moo, administrator at StAG (2004–2010), Program Assistant, Whitworth University, member of Christ The Redeemer, Spokane, Washington, USA.

*****

Although Mark Ashton did not directly lead the youth work at the Round Church and StAG, he came to Cambridge with a heart for discipling young people. The impact of his vision has borne fruit in our own family and in the lives of many other young adults. Knowing even a few of our faults and failings as parents, it has always struck us as utterly miraculous that all three of our children have gone out into the world equipped and willing to serve God. Each of our children was and remains very different but there was a common factor in their spiritual development: the involvement of older Christians who discipled them in their teenage years.

The transition from *Pathfinders* (11–14 year-olds) to *Travellers* (the older teenagers' group) was particularly difficult for two of them. They were acutely aware of being newcomers and felt excluded by the dominant group. We believe that the key contribution to their spiritual growth was made by those assigned to lead mid-week Bible studies. One of the leaders would lead Bible studies with a small group, at a time that suited them all, often immediately following school. Bible study was complemented by social activities: DVDs, meals, outings or, for our daughter, just sharing family life with some young wives and mothers. The leaders were typically in their mid-twenties; young enough to share the same culture but old enough to model mature Christian living. We have kept in touch with many of them and give thanks that in the intervening years they have continued to serve God, moving into positions of paid ministry and church leadership.

Trevor and Janet Rayment, members of the Round/StAG (1980–2008), now at St Ebbe's, Oxford. Trevor is Director of Physical Sciences, Diamond Light Source, near Oxford.

*****

When someone pointed me to an ad for 'Parish Assistants' in Cambridge, it was a new idea to me. Spending a year seeing what church ministry involved while doing practical stuff appealed greatly. My first impressions were all of the eccentric world of Cambridge. But the lasting impression on me is the principle that inglorious service is the first lesson of Christian leadership. That principle had been deeply worked out at StAG. And what a learning curve! One evening, around 10 p.m., I was tracked down at a friend's house by a staff member: I'd forgotten to deliver something. 'Couldn't it wait till morning now?' I asked. Silly question. Or trying to concentrate for my 'study morning' while also answering the phone and doorbell at the church. That made me really cross! But with hindsight, of course – all designed for my godliness.

My fellow PA, Joe, and I still re-enact some of the tellings-off we got from Mark Ashton – once at the full length of the auditorium as people arrived on Sunday morning! But they were not impulsive or mood-driven; they were for our godliness. We always knew that the staff were for us whatever we'd done, and whatever hard words needed saying. One of the real privileges and highlights for me, strangely, was the weekly staff meeting and the occasional staff away days. There I saw how church decisions were thought through. 'Attention to detail' became our bread and butter (arranging chairs, re-photocopying 600 notice sheets...); at the staff meeting the same principle was applied at every level. We had lots of fun that year. Lifelong friendships were forged. But most of all, our future ministries were shaped as nowhere else: we learnt to serve.

Mark Simpson, on the staff as parish assistant and student worker at StAG (1995–2000), Minister, Wellfield Church, Leyland.

*****

From my very first Sunday as a fresher (first year student), I knew that the Round Church would be a mainstay that would not only help me stand firm, but stretch me as a Christian while at Cambridge. I never bothered to try any other churches. It was not even tempting, since it would mean missing a precious Sunday. I will never forget the sermon on that first Sunday – Mark Ashton on the Beatitudes. It was as if the Bible had suddenly become the Himalayas rather than the Cotswold hills. This was 1991, when the Round Church met in the Union Society Building. One of the things that immediately made you feel part of the church family as a whole was that we all faced one another in that august debating chamber, rather than being lined up in pews. Indeed, it was such an encouragement to see others' faces as we worshipped Christ and received his word that this seating layout was preserved when we moved to StAG in 1994, during my last year as an undergraduate.

Above all, I am abidingly grateful for the remarkable emphasis on discipling students by Round Church staff, of which I was a major beneficiary. Having studied the Bible one-to-one with Mary Juckes (now Davis) in my first two terms as a first year, she then continued to meet with me weekly throughout my time as a college Christian Union leader and while on the Cambridge Inter-Collegiate Christian Union exec (the leadership committee). In the end, that meant I met up with her once a week for the whole of my Cambridge career! What an enormous privilege. But the importance of this goes beyond the personal. It was a very tangible expression not only of the Round Church's commitment to the changing needs of individuals, but of its support for and desire to strengthen the student leadership of that era.

I began with my first Sunday, and shall end with my last, when we were given a wonderful acrostic on how to become a spiritual DINOSAUR after Cambridge (D – dire devotional life; I – ignore the cross; N – neglect other Christians; O – observe, don't get involved; S – spend selfishly; A – anonymous discipleship; U – unapplied Christian truth; R – rival to Jesus). It was typical of the fun and humour which always accompanied the imparting of profound wisdom, and made the Round Church a thrilling place to be a student.

Ursula Weekes (née Mayr-Harting), undergraduate at the Round/StAG (1991–94), now housewife and art historian and a member of Emmanuel, Wimbledon.

*****

Under Mark Ashton the 'footprint' of StAG grew exponentially. Not only did he share Mark Ruston's passion, priority and love for the individual, he also had the vision and leadership gifts to multiply his own ministry through the deployment of a substantial staff team. Mark Ashton also recognised that the international nature of Cambridge University gave the work with individuals at StAG a global reach. He often spoke of his expectation that the British undergraduate population of the university would grow progressively less in proportion to that of the overseas undergraduate and postgraduate population. This provided yet another opportunity, in his mind, for the expansion of God's Kingdom through personal discipleship. The famous phrase of 'From Cambridge to the world' was to be achieved, in part, through the world coming to Cambridge.

William Taylor, undergraduate at the Round (1980–83), theological student at Ridley Hall (1988–91), Rector, St Helen's Bishopsgate, London.

*****

Emmanuel Church, Hastings, will always be indebted to Mark for his support of our application to establish partnership links with StAG. For nearly seven years, and I think almost entirely to our benefit, prayer requests, funding and high-calibre Ministry Apprentices were exchanged. At one time of particular turbulence at the local level, knowing we had Mark's support counted for everything.

Philip Coekin, member of StAG while a government on-farms adviser based in Cambridge (1989–93), Vicar of Emmanuel Church, Hastings (2000–11), Vicar of Holy Trinity, Eastbourne since 2011.

*****

I arrived in Landbeach to work as an au-pair. Leaving my home in Prague was an attempt to do away with a dissatisfying life and pursue a better future in the West. My level of English was good enough only to communicate with the ten English Whippet show dogs – friendly members of an otherwise rather cold host family. So I grabbed the first opportunity to socialize with some fellow foreigners at an au-pair party where I was invited to the Barn, a coffee bar. At a Bible study held there I met Stephen Tuck who somehow managed to lower his level of English not only to compliment Czech Beer but also explain to me the key points of one of Jesus' parables. I was so happy by his invitation to his church, St Andrew the Great, and felt very much cared for by his offer to come to Landbeach to pick me up that Sunday morning. My English was too weak to understand much of the sermon but the love and care of the members of the congregation as well as the welcoming hosts of international lunches drew me back. At a low-English Bible study group (*Hub*), I was helped to understand Philippians 2:1–11. Now I know God used it to help me to understand that having Jesus as my Saviour cannot be separated from having Him as my Lord. On the same April day I asked Him to be both, my Saviour and my Lord.

Inner joy and prosperity that followed were broken by a phone call from my father: 'Your brother broke his spine and is fighting for life.' This shook my definition of God's blessings but it was in his good timing that I had just started to live with a Christian family. What I was able to understand of God's grace through the sermons preached at StAG at that time, I daily experienced in the home of this wonderful family. Patiently led one-to-one Bible studies helped my understanding of the magnitude of the gospel and the story of my brother Vašek in its light.

I began to be involved in the gospel ministry among internationals in Cambridge and after further training back in the Czech Republic. Since 2005 I have served as a Travelling Secretary and later General Secretary of the Czech IFES student movement and very much enjoyed bringing the gospel and teaching God's word to Czech students. In StAG I learned and experienced that the word of God does the work of God and that keeps me going in life and ministry to this day.

Tom Uher, at StAG (2001–05), now General Secretary of the Czech International Fellowship of Evangelical Students, Brethren Church, Prague Vinohrady.

*****

I returned to the Round Church congregation in early 1987 (having been there first as an undergraduate) and, as a techie, I was naturally drawn to helping with the video and sound relays for the morning services at the Round and later in the Union Society Debating Chamber. So the practical problems of a congregation too big for its building were very much on my heart.

Although the move to StAG was going to make us a lot more 'outsider-friendly', we could see from the start that it wasn't going to be big enough for the whole congregation to meet together. Mark Ashton occasionally joked that I'd been the one telling us all that we'd need to think about church-planting long before we made the move to StAG, but I'm not sure I remember it that way!

Part of our vision for our church has long been in the way we were helping the wider church by continually sending out leaders. It always seemed important that we should teach and train these brothers and sisters as well as we could to be gospel workers wherever they were going next. A church plant is really the same idea but in rather more concentrated form! Of course the chief distinction is in sending a minister with the plant.

For the first two church plants, to Little Shelford and Christ Church, we remained at StAG and experienced the pain of close friends not being there each week after the move. When the third planting opportunity came around, God was gracious enough to let us go with it. Mark Ashton's advice to us at the commissioning service was that each of us should guard carefully our own walk with God; read our Bibles and pray regularly. There is indeed no more important thing any of us could be doing for the health of our churches.

After twenty-one years at the Round Church and StAG, we really were part of the furniture. What has amazed us is the speed with which we now belong to St Matthew's. I'm quite sure it is by God's grace directly to us, but also over-flowingly through those who were at St Matthew's before we arrived. It is because we are so much a part of each other as fellow believers in Christ that we can be at home together so quickly. A few months after we moved, I had confused myself over evening service times (St Matthew's evening service is half an hour later than StAG's) and arrived very early. So I decided that, as it was only ten minutes away, I'd go the StAG evening service for a change. As it happened, I even sat next to Mark Ashton who had pastored me for so many years and through so much. Here though, I was only a visitor. StAG was already no longer my church, despite so many good friends being present. Though I owe my life to the ministry of the Round Church, under God, I know full well that we now belong at St Matthew's.

Mark Ayliffe, member of the Round/StAG (1982–84, 1987–2008), moved with other StAG members to St Matthew's, Cambridge in 2008, Software Engineer.

*****

I remember my years as an undergraduate at StAG (or the Round Church meeting in the Union Society Debating Chamber, as it was then) with great affection: Mark Ashton's preaching and his personal dynamic ministry were very influential. Several things immediately stand out. First, his preaching was direct, impassioned, no-nonsense, captivating, and full-blooded. I distinctly remember one occasion of his preaching and my feeling as if I was being pinned to the back wall of the Union Chamber. Mark Ashton had, I think, an unusual ability to get to the heart of the matter and bring it home to the heart. Second, his character. He was clearly a model of disciplined and committed Christian living, devoted to his family and to his church. Third, although I didn't really get to know Fiona particularly well, I do remember the home she created when we visited with many other students. It felt like a fully 'Christian' home in the way that's hard to put your finger on but you know when you experience it. Welcoming, charming, but real and Spirit-filled.

Josh Moody, in Cambridge as undergraduate (1987–92) and post-graduate (1994–97), now Senior Pastor of College Church, Wheaton, Illinois.

*****

When Mark Ashton arrived, it was clear that he was going to give plenty of attention to the family service and there were innovations in the way the service was run. When the move to the Union Society came, we were much more confident of our place in the congregation and of how a good family church could provide the basis for a good student church. In the Union, it was great to see the whole church assembled – and their faces too! The children's groups ran in conveniently adjacent rooms. When the time came to move to StAG, I was asked to serve on the committee charged with finding a future for the Round Church building. This proved to be a frustrating, but eventually fruitful, slog over several years, negotiating with the many interested heritage bodies.

Keith and Sarah Haddow, members of the Round/StAG (1982–97), moved with other members of StAG to All Saints, Little Shelford, in 1997. Keith is a financial director and Sarah is a school teacher.

For someone who claimed to loathe consistency as the 'hob-goblin of tiny minds', Mark Ashton was remarkably consistent himself. 'Christ suffered for you, leaving you an example, so that you might follow in his steps', was drilled into his system in such a way that it affected every aspect of his life. Whether Mark had a toilet-duck in his rubber-gloved hands and was vigorously cleaning the downstairs loo on a Saturday morning (with its scores of pictures of family and friends on the walls and hundreds of memory verses in boxes on the windowsill); or was insisting that we attend to the various 'men of the road' when they rang at the vicarage door; or was putting his family first by jealously guarding the sacrosanct time with Fiona, Chris, Clare and Nick; or was throwing you the keys of the car so you could pick up a speaker (he insisted on comprehensive insurance – it was Christ's Volvo, not his); or had his hands in the sink after yet another of Fiona's Sunday feasts that welcomed so many people; or was off to play squash with his regular squash partners, not least so that his evangelism was firsthand; or was...; the list is endless. Above all Mark Ashton was consistently big-hearted: from the way he signed himself with that heart-shaped 'M', through his welcoming but crushing bear-hugs, to his breadth of vision for internationals and the worldwide church. No wonder that Mark left something of an example himself, and lovingly drilled what it meant to follow Christ into those around him.

Jem Hovil, parish assistant at the Round (1989–92), Director of the Entrust grass roots pastor training programme of E3 Initiative working in the global south, based in Cape Town, a leader of Muizenberg Community Church.

*****

Mark Ashton was one of the 'older brothers', training for ordination at Ridley Hall and doing a great ministry of evangelism and encouragement among us undergraduates. You could rely on him for a fresh take on things. Our Christian house party leadership was wondering whether to ban an activity after an accident. 'Youth leadership involves danger!' he insisted, and rock scrambling continued. Mark Ashton combined the unflappable determination of a natural leader with an infectious smile.

John Hutchison, undergraduate at the Round (1971–75), Chaplain, Sheffield Children's Hospital.

*****

My wife Carol had been ill with cancer for a couple of years when Mark announced his own diagnosis to the church. As we left she gave him a hug and said, 'Welcome to the club.' Rather less tactfully, I reminded him of an earlier conversation in which Carol had said how much she was looking forward to having Mark take her funeral, and I suggested that he should try to stay alive a little longer. In the event, Carol died three months before Mark, and he did take both her funeral service and a thanksgiving service in StAG. He was very ill at the time and was seriously exhausted by the end of the day, but Mark never gave any hint that he might want to be doing anything other than spending the day serving his church family. His main response to my letter of thanks was simply to encourage me to push on in my own Christian ministry. I owe him more than I can possibly say.

Peter Robinson, member of the Round/StAG since 1980, Professor of Computer Technology at Cambridge University.

Extracts from personal letters to Mark Ashton

(Quoted with permission)

Because of your faithfulness in teaching God's word clearly, I came to know Jesus as Lord and Saviour. My husband and our daughter are also followers of Jesus now. In fact, Dick and I were recently baptised as believers! As a college professor, I have told many students about God's amazing love and his plan of salvation and some of them have now come to know Jesus as their Lord and Saviour. So you see, Mark, because of your faithfulness, another generation of people will be with you in heaven praising God. I am SO thankful to God for directing my path to the Round Church. I am so thankful to you for your faithful following of his call on your life.

Marilyn Pelosi, member of StAG in 1993 and 2007, now Associate Dean at Western New England University, Springfield, Massachusetts and member of Wellspring Church.

*****

I met you at a summer conference of students for Jesus in Zubri in the Czech Republic. When I was fifteen, I had believed that there is a God and went to the Catholic church. It hadn't worked and I had taken my life back into my hands and went through life on my own. At the beginning of 2006, I hit the bottom of my life: I had nearly achieved everything I wanted in my life and had thought it would make me happy, but I was broken down – burned out, morally down, sad and no sign of happiness. So I went into myself and returned home like a prodigal son. A friend took me to the conference where you were speaking. I could for the first time in my life fully experience God's love from the start of your talk and thanks to your teaching. Someone at the conference helped me to understand that God through his only Son forgave all my sins and we prayed for a short moment and I went to sleep. Next morning, I woke up very early and went to the lake by the camp. The wind was absolutely silenced, no move of the air. The surface of the lake was like a mirror and was reflecting the sky above, so was peace in my heart – no voices pushing me forward, no blaming. First in my life I have been forgiven and forever. Your teaching was great the whole week and I have listened to the recordings many times afterwards. The good seeds you set in my life grow so strong and fruitful, that not whole two years after I have been offered to be a staff member for one year of training in KVZ (now called In-Life). I left the manager career and my home town and followed the calling of Jesus. I am sorry that my English is so bad but I can't help but let you know about the fruit you spread around you. Jesus in you is so big and so clear to understand through the words of your preaching and life.

Lukáš Purm met Mark Ashton at students' conference, now working with In-Life, sharing the love of Jesus with students in the Czech Republic.

*****

I think what I particularly value about your ministry is that you do not care what people think of you and so you say things that no-one else would dare say. That's true in the pulpit but it's also true in conversation.

Paul Bolton, theological student at Ridley Hall (1995–98), working for the Titus Trust, Oxford and member of St Ebbe's Church.

The Round Church (in the Union Debating Chamber) was a lifeline to me when I was caught up in the churchiness of being an organ scholar at Trinity Hall. I remember feeling revived and refreshed and 'breathing clean air' during each service. It was dear Chris Hayward who recruited me to do bits of music and then suggested the 'London Week'[1] for my final Christmas vacation – that set me on the path to full-time service.

Rupert Demery, undergraduate at Cambridge (1991–94), theological student at Ridley (1998–2001), now Chaplain, Eton College.

*****

My time in Cambridge was so spiritually significant for me – both in terms of my personal relationship with Jesus and also in providing me with a model for future ministry. Thank you for your part in that – in your teaching and example and encouragement (and the odd rebuke here and there!).

Joe Dent, undergraduate at StAG (1991–94), member of staff at StAG (1994–96), now Associate Rector at St Nicholas, Sevenoaks.

*****

I would like to thank you for your influence on my life. You are one of the few preachers that has brought tears to my eyes and caused the hair to stand up on the back of my neck as I listened to you expound the Scriptures – a real truth encounter. I remember with fondness you inviting me to the vicarage for Sunday lunch. Your firm stand for Christian orthodoxy I have found inspirational – and as such have sought to contend for the faith in my own ministry and not capitulate to the prevailing liberal tide.

Greg Downes, member of the Round (1991–92), now Director of the Centre for Missional Leadership, London School of Theology, member of Soul Survivor, Watford.

I was not particularly impressed the first time I attended StAG. Having grown up in a Catholic church, it all seemed too irreverent! However, people had been overwhelmingly welcoming and I was acutely aware that the repetition I heard at my previous church meant that I rarely listened to prayers, and certainly didn't mean them. Sermons then became an important jolt for me each week; I knew I had much to learn. As I started to listen, I have no doubt that God used you to speak to me; sometimes just a single sentence from your sermon would reverberate for me, and I came to see faith as a secure gift rather than a daily challenge, thanks to reading the Bible. I am so grateful for the support of a church which placed a Bible in my hands every week and encouraged me to have a look for myself. Perhaps I should be more respectful of your intellect and investment of time in writing sermons, but when you made a passage simple and clear, I was encouraged enough to try reading passages myself. Thank you for the dedication which must have been required for your concise observations. Thank you also for the rebukes. There have been many which I disliked but, by pointing to the Bible, I have definitely learnt a little of the gap between the sinner I am and the perfection of Christ.

Lucy Eastcott, member of StAG (2007–09), financial analyst, member of Dundonald Church, Raynes Park, London.

*****

When I arrived at StAG, I was quite a young Christian, having only been converted about a year and a half before. God certainly used your faithful Bible teaching to grow me in my faith. I remember one of my first weeks at StAG, Simon Scott was preaching on 1 Timothy 2 and I have to say it didn't sit comfortably with me! However, I went away and read the passage over and over for myself and came to realise that, although I might not always like God's way, he does indeed have the best way. I think that was a real turning point for me, as I was taught to sit under God's word at all times, not just when it suited me, and I think that has been one of the greatest lessons I've learnt from your faithful ministry.

Petasha Evans (née Lewis), member of StAG congregation (2001–04), on staff as student worker (2004–07), wife and mum, at All Saints, Crowborough.

Three things in particular strike me about your Christian life and ministry. First, your single-mindedness has been a great challenge and example to me. You always had such a grasp of the gospel and Jesus' hold on your life that you've given yourself over to the work of the gospel at the expense of personal desires, comfort or ambition – with a diary shaped around gospel priorities. I am sure your remarkable capacity for hard work springs from this and from a lovely passion for the Lord Jesus which is evident in the clear love of word ministry you have. It's been a wonderful encouragement for me to see someone who clearly still finds gospel work more thrilling and exciting than anything else after several decades engaged in it. You truly have 'fought the good fight, finished the race and kept the faith' to the very end, and it's a wonderful inspiration to Petasha and me as we look to our futures!

Secondly, I have always been very struck by your refusal to fear men or to seek men's praise. I have noticed this quality in several guises – a willingness to say hard things to people both from the pulpit and in private, a non-'party spirit' which neither blindly follows the conventions or fashionable trends of our constituency, nor writes off everything about those from other circles, and your total lack of personal ambition for fame or an international ministry – which you clearly had the capability to enjoy – in order to give yourself to the work at StAG. I have been greatly challenged by your clear desire to please God and to seek his approval and esteem alone – meaning you've been secure enough to allow staff members to disagree with you and to seek the consensus of the church family.

Thirdly, the way you've conducted your family life has been a wonderful example to me. I've learnt a great deal from how you guard family time and prioritise family commitments, and yet have so generously opened up your house to show hospitality to people. You and Fiona have managed to create an atmosphere at your home which makes it the most warm and fun and lovely place to be – I'm quite sure no-one ever wants to leave! I think you and Fiona have perfectly modelled marriage as a spiritual gift for the sake of other believers.

...I wanted to mention finally how challenged I've been by your reaction and attitude to your diagnosis with cancer. It has been heart-warming to see how much you're looking forward to making the most of every opportunity while you're still on earth, trusting in the Lord's will and goodness and unafraid of death. Your example has challenged me to use my time on earth to the maximum, knowing that life is short and each day is a gift from God.

Rupert Evans, undergraduate at StAG (1999–2002), on staff as student worker (2004–06), now at All Saints, Crowborough.

*****

I remember you telling us as first year students not to worry about missing God's plan by choosing the 'wrong' job or place to live but rather to focus on how we live. You reminded us that God was more concerned with our relationship with him than the geography of our lives. I have certainly had my view of God's plan for my life challenged. I thought I would be overseas for life but am now in Exeter! God has showed me the truth of what you said and I am trying to serve him faithfully here.

Ruth Flanagan (née Harley), undergraduate at the Round (1987–91), on leadership team at Belmont Chapel, Exeter, Race Equality Resource Officer and teacher.

*****

You have been a model of gospel ministry to us. First of all, that was for Helen on her own as she saw the way you opened your home to the members of the youth group in Clapham and put into practice the principles of your book *Christian Youth Work*, to which we both remain indebted. Then, in Cambridge, we had the privilege of seeing a vicarage home in action, particularly when we were involved in helping with Pathfinders there on a Sunday morning. We saw the simplicity in which you lived, your generous hospitality and your godly parenting.

Chris Hobbs, member of the Round (1980–83 and 1988–1991), now Vicar of St Stephen's and St Wulstan's, Selly Park, Birmingham and Helen Hobbs (née Warburton), primary school teacher.

*****

One thing we have found particularly helpful has been that you never complained about the hard work of the ministry – you kept going with gospel goals.

Appendix – personal letters

Angela Howard (née Woods), member of StAG (1987–2000), wife and mum, now at All Saints, Thornton Hough, Wirral.

*****

I was particularly grateful for your ministry at StAG. I always appreciated your thoughtful, real, grounded but uplifting sermons – you truly do have a gift for saying difficult things in a way that doesn't come across as superior or easy, but somehow reflects the love and understanding of the Father whose word you're speaking. I remember a carol service where I honestly felt like God himself was there giving me a massive hug through your words! (Maybe not your aim, but believe me it was needed!) I am also grateful for how you so clearly stuck to the centrality of Jesus and the gospel – it turned my anxious gap-year worry about whether or not I was doing what God wanted from me every second of the day, to an understanding that it's all about what he's done, not what I do.

Laura Imeson, member of StAG (2000–03), doctor in palliative medicine, member of St George's, Stamford.

*****

Perhaps the most important moment in retrospect was your encouragement to put my wife Cleone and the kids first on day one. Something which came very easily at StAG, because your expectation of all of us ordinands was so gloriously low. But it's a great lesson now the expectations are higher and where the temptation so often is to take God's most precious gift to me (my family) for granted.

Valentine Inglis-Jones, theological student at StAG (2004–07), Priest-in-charge Liphook and Bramshott, Hampshire.

*****

I believe that the ministry that God has given you at StAG, over the years, has primarily been one of rooting and building up young Christians in the word of God. Many hundreds and probably thousands of believers will have passed through StAG, having spent three years being faithfully taught how the word of God does the work of God. I have no doubt that for most of these believers, the teaching and modelling of the gospel by you and the other teachers will have been foundational and the source of much strength. I praise God that he has used you in this way and continues to do so until the day he finally calls you home.

Nic Lawrence, member of StAG (2000–08), moved with other StAG members to St Matthew's Cambridge, entrepreneur.

*****

The action of reaching out into the pew and picking up the Bible is the best bit of my life at the Round. Following the sermon in the Bible was a genuine life skill that I learnt as a student and that I carry with me to this day. Because wherever we are and whatever we are up to, it is the Bible that is the unchanging part. ...I firmly believe that it is the firm foundation in the word of God that has kept my Christian life on the right track.

Alistair McNarry, undergraduate (1988–93), member of the Round/StAG (1990–1996), anaesthetist, Edinburgh.

*****

The Round and Mark Ruston's ministry to me were a key influence on my life. I was so glad when you picked up the baton from Mark. I have always rejoiced to hear how the ministry at StAG has flourished as God has used you so greatly. I know too that as a result God will raise up badly needed leaders for the future. You were also someone who spurred my new Christian faith as an undergraduate as I saw someone all out for the Lord.

Charles Marnham, undergraduate at the Round (1970–73), Vicar of St Michael's, Chester Square, London.

*****

One thing that I do greatly miss is the 'Grill the Preacher' sessions that ran after the evening service, every once in a while. I had many of my questions answered there, and was comforted by your compassion and sensitivity in your answers.

Gemma Purcell (née Caddy), postgraduate at StAG (2001–04), Cornerstone Church, Nottingham, Clinical Scientist.

Appendix – personal letters

I want to say how eternally grateful I am for my years at StAG. Your sermon on my first Sunday in Cambridge (it was on Ecclesiastes) was the first expository Bible teaching I had ever heard and completely bowled me over. The experience of delight at hearing God's word taught was repeated again and again in my four years with you, and the result was that I went from being an enthusiastic but clueless fresher (first year student) to someone with a far clearer knowledge of the Bible and how to handle it, and a far deeper commitment to wholehearted discipleship. ...The model of ministry and pastoral work, and more importantly, simply of taking and serving Christ seriously, are ones which I pray that I shall go on trying to emulate for the rest of my life.

You said in a sermon once that every time you and Fiona broke something at home, you reminded each other that that was what it was made for and didn't get upset about it. Approximately two hours later in your house I dropped and broke a jug which you had given to Fiona the day before – and your reaction was absolutely in line with your sermon. Another time, you wrote to me after you interviewed me in a service about a year after I had graduated. You thanked me, genuinely, for what I had said – but then took the opportunity to warn me sternly against relying on my natural confidence and neglecting careful, biblical preparation. It is advice which still echoes in my mind with every sermon, talk or Bible study I prepare.

Matthew Roberts, undergraduate at StAG (1993–96), on the staff as parish assistant (1996–97), now Minister, Trinity Church, York.

*****

Our time at StAG was really formative for both of us and part of the reason we now want to spend our lives in gospel ministry is due to the teaching we received there. We often praise God for your faithful ministry over so many years, and many of our friends do the same.

David Rowbory, undergraduate at StAG (1997–2000) and Julie Rowbory (née Magill), undergraduate (1996–2000), with Wycliffe Bible Translators in Jos, Northern Nigeria, members of NKST (Church of Christ among the Tiv), Anglo Jos and of St George's Tron, Glasgow.

I'd not found the transition from undergraduate to research student an easy one. ...You diagnosed my problem – that I needed to be involved in church ministry and you suggested 'The Travellers'. ...It soon became clear that *Travellers* was the name of the youth group. I readily signed up. It was a life-changing decision. Being under Auriel Schluter's guiding hand on Sunday nights, as well as your sermons on a Sunday morning, was inspirational. ...And meeting in the debating chamber of the Union building showed us what 'church' is – the idea of watching each other by looking across the chamber spoke powerfully to us.

Andy Schofield, member of the Round/StAG (1989–99), now Professor of Theoretical Physics, University of Birmingham, member of St Stephen's and St Wulstan's, Selly Park, Birmingham.

*****

I had the opportunity to sit under the faithful preaching of the word at the Round for some eight years. By God's grace, I had understood from the faithful way that the word was opened and expounded, that the grace of God was for me, touched me in all aspects and ways, and should flow out through me. I remember too very vividly your probing one-to-one questions, which I still ask myself today, hearing your voice 'What did you learn in your quiet time today?'

Philip Shipway, member of the Round (1986–95), now Professor of Engineering at the University of Nottingham and a member of Cornerstone Church, Nottingham.

*****

I wanted to take the time to thank you for how God has used you to be a blessing to me. The first time I ever heard you preach was when I was sixteen and visiting my brother in Cambridge. I distinctly remember three things. Firstly, you said that 'our attitude to God's word is our attitude to God'. Jonah had rejected God's word and therefore rejected God. About a year before, I had been quite diligent in reading the Bible, but at that point it had tailed off. As you spoke, I knew that the fact I was ignoring the Bible showed that I was ignoring God. It was probably the first time I knew that I was a sinner (though at that time I didn't have the vocabulary to explain it). The second thing I remember reinforced the first thing. We had read the Bible passage before, but as you preached, you re-read every single part of the passage at least once, in most cases twice. It was only the second time I've ever seen someone take the Bible so seriously (the other instance being my dad in his daily devotions) and the first time I've seen someone behind the pulpit take the Bible so seriously. Such an example made a deep impression on me, and I hope to emulate it in my own ministry. The third thing I distinctly remember was you saying the whale in Jonah was a red herring. But I won't carp on about this one. I look back to that service, and to your talk, as one of the primary means that God used to save me. You have also been very influential in my Christian growth. My decision to apply to Cambridge was entirely based on the fact that I knew there was a good church there, and the four years of faithful teaching I had in my time in Cambridge will have made more of an impact on me than I will ever know.

Josh Vasby-Burnie, member of StAG (1999–2003), mission partner with StAG since 2003, student at Oak Hill Theological College and member of St Helen's Bishopsgate.

*****

I recall the extraordinary value of the times we spent together with open Bibles in my early Christian days. I still use some of the same passages we studied when I manage to meet up with a young believer here and I invariably find that the thing that helps them most is when I stop prattling on about how I see life, and just bury their nose in the word. ...You have been assiduous in remembering, and writing to me on, my spiritual birthday – and I'm not sure I've ever acknowledged that: so let me say how very grateful I have, in fact, always been, and what an encouragement it has been to me to know that you remember, and give thanks, and pray.

Giles Walter, undergraduate at the Round (1972–76), Curate at the Round (1986–93), now Vicar of St John's, Tunbridge Wells.

I arrived a rather conceited, selfish and uncommitted person. That you saw something in me that was worth developing and training will forever be both a mystery and source of huge thankfulness to God. Learning to teach the Bible carefully and practically, understanding leadership as a call to servanthood, and sharing Jesus with others by passing on what had been given to me, were all brought to life by God through your friendship and discipleship. And somehow it was accomplished amidst a huge amount of fun and laughter.

Rick Williams, friend of Mark and Fiona Ashton from St Stephen's, Clapham Park; Associate National Director, Vineyard Churches UK.

*****

I want to say how hugely grateful Ursula and I are to you both for your faithful and fruitful ministry at the Round Church at StAG. I came up as a converted but clueless first year in October 1991. Within forty-eight hours, Richard James had visited me and invited me to the Round. And so on my first Sunday (on which I first met Ursula!) and for all the Sundays during term for the next three years, I came to the Round and was transformed by your ministry there. I think it would be fair to say that I had never heard consistently God-exalting expository preaching before I came to the Round. Sitting under it for three years was profoundly influential and a great privilege, and the fruit of it is still being borne today. It wasn't just Mark's preaching that was so life-transforming. It was the way you opened up your home to us. ...The fun, food and hearty fellowship with friends and family have long since remained in my memory and were a highlight of my years in Cambridge. Now that we try and do the same, we realise just how much work that must have been for Fiona. So thank you for sharing not only the gospel but your lives as well.

Robin Weekes, undergraduate at the Round/StAG (1991–94), now teaching at the PT Cornhill Training Course in London, at Emmanuel, Wimbledon.

Endnotes

1. A programme for students considering full-time paid gospel ministry, run by the Cornhill Training Course in London.